AF322661

GROWING UP GRITS

(Memoir of a <u>G</u>irl <u>R</u>aised <u>I</u>n <u>T</u>he <u>S</u>outh)

By

Ruby Banks Allen

Hardcover ISBN: 9798860592186

Winn Publications LLC, Florida
winnpublications.com

Dedication

This Memoir is dedicated to the matriarch of our family -- the Shero, prayer intercessor, teacher, physician, virtuous woman, chaste keeper at home, Madear -- Mother Anna Lee Banks. With her humble spirit and hard work, she demonstrated good character, impeccable work ethics, and grand devotion to her God and her family. She laid a solid foundation on which we could build and still inspires us to be the best that we can be. Again, her devotion to God and love for her family never ceased; therefore, her memories will live on forever.

Much love Madear

Table of Contents

Introduction

What prompted me to attempt to write a book?

In discussions with my daughter, grandchildren, nieces, and nephews, I found that there were many things that they had never heard of or did not understand what it was like growing up during my childhood years and especially growing up in the South during that period. With the conveniences and inventions that have modernized things and the technology of today, they had a hard time even contemplating that it had not been that long (yes---during my lifetime) when conditions in the South were very different from what they exist today.

Who cares about life in the South or what a young girl thought about it? maybe nobody, hopefully somebody. First, I hope it provides a bit of history for my family and others of life as we knew it growing up in the South and instills an appreciation for the sacrifices made so that they can enjoy the privileges they have today. Secondly, I hope it serves as a testimony of the relationships God has allowed us (family and friends) to enjoy.   Finally, I hope it serves as a conduit to share a legacy of faith which shows God's wisdom from one generation to another, equips them for the tasks set before them, and helps them enjoy God's work in their own lives.

This memoir is not meant to garner sympathy for a victim, but rather to celebrate an overcomer. Prayerfully it will encourage our young people, and the older ones who have forgotten, to be thankful from where God has brought us and to have a courageous faith and consistent trust in Him. It is important to me that this documentation be done while everybody is of sound mind and body.

Chapter 1:

Trip Down Memory Lane (Part 1)

The year 1953 proved to be a grand year!! During that year, Queen Elizabeth II was crowned Queen of England, Jonah Salk and his family got the polio vaccine, Dwight D. Eisenhower was inaugurated as President of the United States, Joseph Stalin died, the average annual wage was $4,000, and the cost of a gallon of gasoline was 20 cents. I love Lucy and the Lone Ranger were popular television shows and Tony Bennett and Nat King Cole topped the music charts. The grandest event of that year happened in the month of December. A young farmer and his wife were blessed to welcome another GRITS (Girl Raised in the South) into their already large family in central Mississippi. The 6th of 13 children, this baby girl would face many challenges, experience the love and loss of many, and thrive in the midst of adversity in the deep South as she grew up in Mississippi.

Living in the South at that time was challenging for everyone, but especially for farmers, the poor, Black people, and large families. Jim Crow laws in the South dictated limitations on what could and could not be done, how it could be done, and who could and could not do certain things. It would be years before The Civil Rights Act was passed in an effort to try to ensure equal rights for all people regardless of race, color, or creed. Many protests would be made and many lives would be lost trying to gain that measure of freedom. It would be many more years before integration of the races would even begin. Only by the grace of God, strong faith, and the resilience of two hard-working parents did we survive and thrive.

Life on the farm could be very hard. Those southern summers were extremely hot, steamy, and stifling, but work on the farm still had to be done. There was a tilling season, a planting season, and a harvesting season. Each had to be done promptly during its season to ensure a sustainable crop. One of my sisters often remarked that if only mother Eve had not eaten that apple, we would not have to work so hard in the fields. Since many people at that time consumed a lot of the vegetables and goods they produced on the farm, it was imperative that everything possible was done to achieve the very best crop yield. Since we were not blessed to have an air conditioner, we spent a lot of our free time under shade trees, slept with the windows open, sat on the porch, and waved that church fan back and forth to try to stay cool.

In the South, many of us experienced growing up in a village. The family consisted of our parents, aunts & uncles, grandparents, cousins, adult neighbors, teachers, church mothers, deacons, preachers, etc. Our neighbors were like family, even if they were not related; most of them actually were related in one way or another. A child could be disciplined by almost any adult when they were caught doing something wrong. If disciplined by a non-parent/neighbor and word got back to the actual parents, often there was a second disciplinary action (many times a whooping) that took place by the parents of that child. In the same sense as with discipline, non-parents/neighbors looked out for, protected, and loved children as if they were their own.

For some reason, our house became and remained throughout my lifetime a gathering place. I don't know if it was because there were so many children at our house to play with or because of my mama's great cooking or her generous sharing, but they came and they stayed. Other parents knew their children were safe at our house and the kids knew my parents didn't play.

Both my parents had a limited education, but they always desired more for their children. We were encouraged to excel in school, even though many days during the planting and harvesting seasons we were picked up from school at noon so we could go home to work in the field. Some of our friends were not allowed to attend school at all during certain seasons of the year. Many of them fell behind in their studies, and some even dropped out of school as a result. In addition to education and farm work, we were instructed and encouraged to develop a personal relationship with God by attending church every Sunday, studying the Bible, singing gospel/ spiritual songs, and living a Godly life.

Although I did not know any wealthy people, I witnessed everyday people sharing as if they were rich. Families, neighbors, and friends shared what they had with those who had less than them or who had nothing. When vegetables were produced, they were shared; when hogs or cattle were slaughtered, packages of meat were shared with family and neighbors. Mind you, there were people of that day who did not share and only looked out for themselves and their families and there were those who exhibited a "better than everybody else" attitude, but that was the exception and not the norm in our area.

Deciding what to eat for any meal was never a decision made by the children. Meals were prepared and we ate whatever Madear put together for that day. During the summer months, we knew that fresh vegetables were on the menu pretty much every day. The meat (entrée) was slim, but we always got full. If you waited too late, you might find that everything had been eaten and there was nothing left for you --- so, we made sure we were on time when the meal was ready. The standing joke was, "If you don't come to eat when you are told it is ready, you might come up behind the light house."

For many of my growing-up years, locking windows and doors was not something most people were concerned about. The wooden latches that locked most doors then would not be considered deterrents these days. Not that everybody was honest and there weren't any unsavory characters around; there definitely were and most people knew who they were. Windows were left open at night and doors were left open during the day. Porch chairs were even turned upside down when the homeowner left home to indicate that no one was at home. Occasionally when a wild animal (bear, panther, bob cat, etc.) or a rabid animal had been sighted, everybody could be seen batting down the hatch and securing windows and doors.

Spring cleaning was a big deal in the South and a big deal at our house. Even our not-so-well-insulated house had to be cleaned from top to bottom. That meant windows had to be washed, floors had to be scrubbed, cabinets had to be cleaned, the yard had to be raked/ scraped/brushed, and even under the house had to be cleaned. Cotton-stuffed bed mattresses were empties of their content, the beds were sprayed for possible bed bugs, the covers washed, mattress content aired out and then refilled, and bed freshly made. Quilts and/or blankets had to be washed and put away.

In our family, every member was assigned responsibilities – I won't call them chores because they were more than chores: they were unpaid jobs! When you live on a farm, even the small children have jobs to do. Everything from housework, to working in the fields, to taking care of the farm animals became everybody's job. Assigned tasks were generally delegated according to appropriate age, but there were no slackers. To this day I remain thankful for the strong foundation that was instilled, the work ethic, the moral character, and the desire to make a better life for myself and my family.

Even though we lived well below the poverty level, and we didn't have some things others had, I don't think we fully understood that we were poor. Many of our friends and neighbors were in the same situation we were, barely eking out a living on their farm. I don't ever remember missing a meal --- even though there were days the food was not what I, as a child, would have preferred to eat. I was and am still thankful that I realized my parents did the best they could with what they had to work with.   My mama was unsurpassed in her skills at stretching a meal to feed her crew and at adapting recipes to accommodate what she was preparing --- and it was always so good. From a hearty breakfast every morning to the pot of spaghetti with red wieners, we ate well.

Every family in the neighborhood had their own deep well as there were no public water lines at that time. The deep wells served as the source of our water supply – water for drinking, water for bathing, water for cooking, water for washing clothes, etc. A long cylinder metal well bucket suspended by ropes (or chains in some cases) guided through a pulley was dropped down the well, allowed to fill with water, pulled up, and poured into a pail. A long handle dipper was used to dip water from the pail for drinking. When water was needed for other things, this drawing process was repeated several times until the required amount of water was drawn. This task was delegated to the children of the household. The rule of the house was that whoever drank the last dipper of water had to draw the next bucket of water to replenish the pail. Needless to say, a lot of people tried to ease that dipper back into an empty bucket as quietly as possible to avoid having to draw that next bucket. Certain members of the family became infamous for doing this. Unthinkable today, but back then everybody drank water from the same dipper and then put it back into the pail of drinking water with no thought of sanitation or spreading germs.

Living and working on a farm, sweating, and getting dirty was the way of life. Therefore, soap and water were very much necessary to maintain clean bodies and clean clothes. Since most families, like ours, did not have running water in my early years, a #3, galvanized steel tub or a smaller foot-tub was the "bathtub" of that day. A white wash basin/pan was used for lighter wash-ups or face washings. Not taking a bath was not an option with the number of people we had in our house and in such close quarters. The air could quickly sour if someone forgot this daily task --- and everybody would quickly point out the offending person.

Washing dishes was a task assigned to the girls of the household. Water was boiled on the gas stove supplied by a 25-gallon upright bottle of gas, or a wood heater, and dishes were washed and towel-dried before being put away after each meal. There were no dirty dishes left until the next day. There were no dish drains in my early years in which to put dishes in for overnight drying. As each of the six girls got old enough, we took turns washing the dishes. We were always checking to make sure everybody had taken a turn before it got back around to us. Of course, there was always somebody forgetting that it was their turn or trying to get away with not doing dishes.

In addition to getting water from the deep well, large Number 3 tubs were placed at the edge of the house to catch rainwater. This water could be boiled and used for bathing, washing clothes, washing dishes, and moping floors. It was not a source of drinking water or cooking water. As a large family, we used a lot of water for bathing and cleaning; therefore, when we were able to catch a tub of rainwater, that was one less tub of water we had to draw from the well.

Before the days of running water and a washing machine, and because of the size of our large family, we often took a black pot (I still own one) in which to boil water, the number three tubs in which to wash and rinse clothes, and all those dirty clothes to my uncle's pond which was located in his pasture. There we got water from the pond and brought it to a boil in the black pot. We washed our clothes by hand, using a scrub board and lye soap that my mama had made. This was hard work, but it got the clothes clean and fresh. We then hung them on the barbed-wire fence surrounding the pasture to dry. Later that day, we went back to the pond\pasture to retrieve the dry clothes.

Years later, when we got a washing machine and running water, clothes were washed at home or taken to the local laundromat and then hung on homemade clotheslines or fences near the house to dry. We always had several lines of clothes to hang to dry on wash days. Some days it became a race to get the dry clothes from the lines before a pop-up rain shower wet them again. When we first got that washing machine (the wringer type where you fed the clothes through the wringer to press the water out of them), we were delighted to have it but not exactly familiar with the proper operation. One day, while trying to put clothes through the wringer, my sister Eva's hand got sucked into the wringer. It continued to roll, pulling her hand in first, then her arm, rolling completely up to the armpit ---- and it continued to roll on her arm when it could go no further. We didn't know what to do and, of course, we were scared. Thankfully my cousin Chuck (Charlie Babe) was passing by and knew what to do. He pressed the release button on the side of the machine to stop the wringer and release it. She was able to slide her arm out. With no serious injury, but a life-long scar, she was okay. To this day, that cousin swears he saved her life!

Another task assigned to the girls was ironing --- yes, ironing all the clothes, ours and all the boys' clothes. Ironing blue jeans for six boys for school was a major job all by itself. Throw in their shirts and your own personal clothes and you could be ironing the better part of a day. In addition, cleaning the house, mopping the floors, cooking, and washing dishes were jobs assigned to the girls. Everybody had to make their own beds though. Leaving a bed unmade was unacceptable in our house.

You were expected to make that bed even on days you had to go to the field very early in the morning or before the school bus came on school days. I still feel compelled to make my bed almost as soon as I get out of it. Making the bed daily just makes the room look neater/cleaner.

Thankfully, the boys had the job of plowing the field, with a mule in the early years and later with a tractor, slopping the hogs, feeding the mule, and cutting down, loading by hand, and hauling pulp wood. Cutting down the trees and splitting the wood for the fireplace and wood heaters were mainly the boys' job too. Before daddy bought a power saw, the cutting down and cutting into block-size pieces to be split for use in the heater and fireplace was done with a buck saw/crosscut saw or a cross bow saw. While the boys cut down the trees and did most of the splitting, once the tree was done and dragged to the house, both boys and girls manned the saws to cut the trees/limbs into appropriate length pieces. Stacking the wood was everybody's job as well as bringing some wood into the house to start and keep a fire going all day. I remember going into the woods on some cold wintry days to gather kindling (lighted knot or lout-utt knot) to start fires when the weather was extremely cold. Working in the freezing conditions to collect the kindling, we sometimes felt like our hands, fingers, and feet were frost-bitten. Thankfully, none of us ever lost a toe or a finger. Somehow, we made it!!

During my younger years, we did not have a gas heater, only a wood-burning heater in the kitchen and a fireplace in the family room. Every child who was "old enough" took a turn making the fire in the chimney and wood heater on cold mornings. This had to be done to heat the house before the others got up to get dressed. Since this was the source of heat for the family, it was done regardless of weekdays and weekends, before school, and/or before going to the field. In a house not well insulated, this was a necessity. We were taught how to place the kindling under the wood, and soak it all in kerosene (occasionally gas, if you knew what you were doing), and light-it-up without getting burned or burning the house down.

Another not-so-pleasant job was that of bringing-in at night and taking-out in the morning the family slop-jar. For those of you who don't know what that is, it's an enamel bucket with a lid (portable toilet) that we used at night. Everybody hated this job. With a large family using the pot, we had to have a big slop-jar – BUT that one would get full overnight. The person lucky enough to be the one taking it out in the morning had to do so very carefully, not just because it was full of urine but just in case someone had an upset stomach during the night. Thankfully that didn't happen often. The slop jar then had to be washed out and left to dry and air-out all day. The day that running water and indoor plumbing came to our house was a much-welcomed blessing.

With a 3-bedroom house and a growing family, where did everybody sleep? Well, our parents had a room, the girls had one bedroom, and the boys had one bedroom. We were stacked three people to a full-size bed. While that may seem crowded now, at that time I did not think so. I fondly remember the stories we told each other at night, the games we played, and snuggling under the cover to keep warm in the wintertime. One of my bed mates had a habit of telling us to quickly pull the cover over our heads so she could tell us a secret. We were so gullible that we fell for that stunt over and over again.

Well, once we got under the cover, she would let go a loud and smelly fart as she passed gas and then laughed at us for being fooled again. I also remember waiting for one of the others to go to bed first so their body heat could start warming the bed during the winter months.

I don't remember an awful lot about the first house we lived in, but I do remember it did not have a ceiling – you could look past the rafters above to view the black tar paper directly under the tin roof. The walls had no insulation, with only one side completed. The floor had only one layer of wide planks and not every plank touched the next. Literally, things could fall through the cracks, and you could see the chicken under the house. I remember as a child thinking how convenient it was to just sweep the dirt from the floor right out the cracks and not have to pick it up.

In my early years, we were blessed to build a new 4-bedroom house – thank the Lord!!! The old house was torn down to make room for the new one. The family temporarily moved to the vacant house of a former neighbor who had moved to the city. I don't remember a lot about our time at that house, but I do remember being afraid all the while we lived there—and I don't even remember why. During this displacement, this new house was going up. We did not have a professional company or strangers building the house: my parents, siblings, and I built it. I remember using a hammer and carrying supplies for use in building the new residence. With the 4-bedrooms, the girls still had one bedroom, but it was a large room with multiple beds, the boys had two bedrooms, and our parents still had their bedroom. Our new house had a ceiling and a double floor with no more cracks or holes in the floor. A front porch the length of the house was the icing on the cake. The porch was later screened-in, and we enjoyed gathering there during our growing up years and into our adulthood up until the house burned down.

Hair care was not always a pleasant task but somehow Madear, mastered it and later we learned to master it as well. Unlike the depiction of little black girls you see in the movies and on television during this time period, my mama made sure our hair was groomed every day. All my sisters had long, flowing black hair; however, I inherited a sandy brown, short grade of hair. Because of the length of my hair, I was not blessed to be able to wear the ponytail style hairdos others had but I sported my braids or plaits as we called them then. I remember the reference to the slow, flowing hymn, "Swing Low, Sweet Chariot" sung with longer hair and the fast, choppy song, "Little Daivd Play on Your Harp" sung with short hair as a demeanor or put-down of girls with short hair. Where my mama got the strength and energy to do all those heads (six girls) every day, especially before school, I will never understand. We did not have all the fancy oils, shampoos, and other hair care products. Our hair was shampooed with soap (generally Ivory soap or P & G soap). Water for shampooing was drawn, heated, and put in a basin for washing and then for rinsing. Our hair dressing was that little white and red box of Royal Crown hair dressing. It did the job and left the hair looking and smelling good.

Pressing or straightening hair was the style of the day. As such, our Saturdays were designated as hair-straightened day. That straightening comb was heated on the wood heater, and later the gas stove, and believe me it got hot. It was very important that we remained still and made no sudden moves, especially when straightening the nape area (we called it the kitchen). Nobody wanted to get burned on the ear, neck, and/or forehead, although we all got it more than once and probably many, many times when we were learning to do our own hair. If you were old enough or lucky enough to get curls, you had to endure a heated curling iron in the same way.

Daddy took the boys to get their hair cuts. His brother-in-law, Maskar Walters, we called him Uncle Boy, was the local barber. Unlike our Saturday adventure with the straightening comb, the boys almost always got their hair cut early on Sunday mornings – and still made it to Sunday School or Church on time.

Before refrigerators were widely used, homeowners would purchase a large, rectangular-shaped block of ice placed in a croker sack. Pieces of ice were chipped off this block with which to cool off things and people.

Store bought brooms were few and far between. We made straw brooms from natural straw which we used to sweep the house. When the straw was dry, we would go to areas (called straw patches) where the straw grew tall and cut enough to make several brooms at a time. The straw was cut about 4-5 feet long and the stacks brought back to the house where the excess straw was trimmed away. A broom about three to five-inches in diameter was made by tying straw together with strings, twine, or strips of torn rags or whatever was available, wrapped around every few inches to hold the straw in place. The brooms did a good job of sweeping clean the wooden floors.

Just like store-bought brooms were few and far between, so was a store-bought rake. Like many of the people in our community, we went into the woods and cut branches ranging from 5-8 feet long, tied several together with strings, twine, or strips of old rags and used these "brush brooms" to clean or rake the yards. In addition to keeping the yard clean regularly, at least once a year these brush brooms were used to brush or rake under the house. We had chicken and dogs that roamed freely and often took shelter under the house so that was not a pleasant task. But, when we were finished, it was a nice, cool place to sit for short periods of time.

Other than working in the fields, the girls of the family rarely worked outside the home. The owner of the local chicken farm occasionally came by to see if the boys in the community, including my brothers, wanted to catch chickens at night to load them into trucks when it was time to sell them. The boys had a window of opportunity to earn a little extra cash and often took advantage of it, even on a school night.

Chapter 2:

Down on the Farm

HOG KILLING

There were many jobs on the farm that were done during a specific time of the year. Hog killing was one of those jobs which was done when the weather was cooler. This was a family job (and sometimes a community job) because the weight of the animal and the amount of processing to be done required strength and lots of man-hours. Before the killing, a hog that had reached the desired size was removed from the general herd, placed in a separate pen, and fed (fatted) specifically to clean them out. Once this was achieved, he was ready for the chopping block.

A big black pot of water was kept boiling throughout the day for use in the whole process. Our daddy used a 50-gallon drum with boiling water, anchored to the ground at an angle by huge, wooded stakes in which to submerge the slaughtered hog for a short period of time. This was done so that the skin could be softened to remove the hair. Since only about half the hog would fit in the drum at a time, one end was dunked, the hog pulled out, and then the other end dunked. While one end was submerged, we were busy pulling the hair from the other end of the hog that had just came out of the boiling water. Then we repeated it with the other end. Even after the hog was pulled from the water, sometimes there was still hair that had to be splashed with hot water and even scrapped with a knife to ensure that it was clean.

A pulley with chains, secured between two trees, was then used to pull the hog into the air by the hind legs until it had completely cleared the ground. Once in the air, a very sharp butcher knife was used to make a cut from top to bottom, allowing the entrails to fall into the number 3 galvanized tub placed beneath it. The hog was then washed several times before being taken down from the pulley and placed on a table for processing. Several strong people were needed to transfer the hog between the drum, pulley, and finally the processing table. As children, we were not involved in the major processing of the hams, shoulder, belly, head, feet, etc. but everybody that was big enough to wield a knife was put to cutting once the big portions had been separated. We were happy to use the meat grinder to grind some of the meat into sausage. However, first we were relegated to cleaning the entrails/intestines/chitterlings. This is the very reason I do not eat, nor do I like the smell of chitterlings today. At least two tubs of water were used for the cleaning process – one for washing and one for rinsing. Once the waste was removed, we filled the casings/chitterlings with water several time, washing them thoroughly until they were clean. Some of these chitterlings were put aside for my daddy to eat and some were used for casings for stuffing sausages. Meat was placed in a grinder which was attached to a table. The grinder had a handle which we turned to grind meat that was placed into the wide mouth opening. As the meat was ground, it was forced out of the grinder through another section and caught in a bowl. Various spices and seasonings were added to the sausage meat after it was ground and before it was stuffed into the casings using another part of the grinder machine. Some of these sausages were eaten right away and most were strung up in our smokehouse to let dry before consumption.

The skin was cut away from the meaty parts of the hog. It was then cut into strips and then smaller pieces which were cooked in hot oil in the black pot where they became pork skins or pork rinds. Cracklings were also a by-product of the cooked skin and were used to make that famous, Southern crackling bread.

Serving portions of meat were placed in wax-like, white butcher paper and sealed. Portions were placed in the smoke house to "cure" or dry before use. Packs of various parts of the hog were set aside for sharing with family, neighbors, and friends. Hog-killing was often a community blessing, not just one family.

THE FOWL SIDE

A favorite task to any child raised on the farm was gathering eggs. Because we were a large family, chickens and eggs were staples of our family meal. Therefore, we raised lots of chicken, some for eating and some for supplying the eggs needed for breakfast, baking, etc. Daddy built a wooden hen-nest/chicken coop about five feet off the ground with separate sections/cubicle-type spots to accommodate 3-5 hens since we had several hens that were laying eggs daily. I liked feeding the chicken but did not like for them to jump on me. My sister Stella could be run out of the county if a chicken was place on her because of her fear of them. I did not fear them, but just didn't want them on me. I remember standing at the bottom of the nest waiting for the eggs to drop. If we saw an egg drop, we would sometimes run the hen off the nest and collect the egg before the eggshell had time to harden.

I don't know how my mama knew when a hen was ready for setting or brooding (sitting on eggs to hatch them), but somehow she knew. My sister thinks it was when the hen stopped clucking. I didn't realize they ever stopped. Sometime the hen didn't want to get off the eggs and we would leave them for her to "set" or she would go away from the home-made hen-nest and lay eggs in other places in the yard or sometimes in the woods. She sat upon those fertilized(?) eggs for a period of time until they hatched, producing baby chicks. We quickly learned that you do not mess with a mother hen with baby chicks because she would "flog" or fight you in defense of her little ones. Those mama hens took their charge serious and took care of their babies and they would fight man or animal to defend them. For the most part, our chickens were free-range. Occasionally we had a chicken pen. When they escaped the pen, we had to chase them down to get them back to the pen, especially that mama hen and her chicks.

Every Southerner knows that many a Sunday Dinner included fried chicken. Since we raised our chicken, they had to be killed and processed before that dinner came to be. Madear would catch a chicken by the neck, swing it around in a circular motion until the neck was broken. Once the chicken was dead, the feathers were removed, usually by the children, using boiling water. Then the bird was cut open, insides removed, washed, and cut into pieces for cooking. Each child had a specific piece of chicken that we ate. My piece then and still is the leg or drumstick. My sister Maxine always referred to her piece as "the last piece that goes over the fence" or the back/butt part. I think she may have graduated from that piece now. Several of my classmates shared that no piece of the chicken was wasted in their family. They remembered using chicken feet to make chicken stew (chicken and dumplins) and for frying, even though there actually was no meat on them. Well, I don't remember cooking or eating the feet at our house thank the Lord, but I have to admit I don't know what everybody ate.

Since Sunday dinner often included fried chicken and most preachers were known to enjoy a piece or two, some families would invite them to share their Sunday meal. I don't remember ever having a preacher (other than family members) join us for that meal. I don't know if they felt sorry for us or knew that they would be limited in how much they could eat if they came to our house. A few people in the community, fellow preachers or those with few or no children, were known to host them.

DAIRY AS WE KNEW IT

We weren't dairy farmers, nor did we have a herd of cattle, but we did have a cow and a calf at one time. Uncle Barney always had cows (who produced calves) so there were cows to be milked often ---- and Madear wound up doing a lot of the milking. Cows are milked by machines today, but we were the milkers back in those days. I never really mastered the art of milking mainly because I was afraid the cow was going to kick me, and I could not pull the teat/udder hard enough to make the milk flow down in a steady stream. Madear could do it with ease and finesse all while putting the cow at ease, so she stood there and allowed her to milk her. Once the calf had finished nursing, the cow was tied up, the udders washed with warm, soapy water and rinsed, and the milk pulled into the waiting pail. Some of the milk was for drinking. Some was set aside allowing the cream to rise to the top, where it was skimmed off to make butter. There is nothing in the world that compares to freshly churned butter. The churn we used was a 2–3-gallon ceramic stoneware container with a removable top that had a hole in the middle where a wooden paddle with a "x" shape at the bottom went through it.   Once the cream was added to the churn, the handle put through the hole, and the lid put in place, the churning process began. I don't remember how long it took, probably 20-30 minutes, but I remember pushing the handle up and down until the butter began to form and rise to the top. It was then skimmed off and stored or used in cooking and eating. The milk left after making the butter was buttermilk. Some family members preferred buttermilk to whole or sweet milk, especially mixed with hot cornbread – a Southern treat. For most of us, whole milk with the cornbread was the preferred treat. Don't knock it if you have not tried it.

Farm animals (ours and the neighbors) were kept in pens, the barn/crib area, or fenced-in pastures. From time to time, parts of the fence or pen would rot or if someone left the gate open, the animals would escape. Uncle Barney had quite a few head of cattle. Occasionally, his animals (cattle, mules, and hogs) would go for a stroll on their own and we had to help herd them back into the pasture. I guess they got tired of being confined and decided to make a run for it. Everybody was called in to chase and/or catch the animals and return them where they belonged. We got our exercise chasing many creatures over the years. Sometimes we had to run down the road or through the woods to stop them. It was a bit scary for me trying to herd that angry cow or bull that did not want to be fenced in back through the gate and back into the pasture. It did not matter whether the animal was ours or our neighbors, if it got out and came our way, we had to try to help capture it.

SWINE TIME

We had a hog pen and usually had 2-3 pigs/hogs at a time. If we didn't have a sow that bred some pigs, daddy would purchase a pig and fatten it up over a period of time till it was time to "make meat". If a sows delivered a litter, there were usually several piglets to feed and grow into hogs for reproducing or for consumption.

The task of feeding or "slopping" the hogs was assigned to the boys in the family. Occasionally, the girls had to pitch in. It was everybody's job to clear their plates of leftovers in a bucket designated for food for the hogs. In addition to our leftovers and stored corn that we raised, daddy purchased "wheat short" for the hogs. It came in large sacks and was made of leftover particles of bran, germ, and flour produced during the milling process. It was a near-powder mixture. This was combined with water to make food that was fed to the hogs. Generally a five-gallon can was used to combine the mixture which was then carried to the eagerly waiting creatures.

The hog food was placed in a wooden trough that daddy built. Feeding time could be a circus; they would run over you if you didn't get the food to them promptly. Sometimes the feeders could barely get the slop over the fence or into the trough before they were pushing each other out of the way or trying to climb up the pen to reach it. When they escaped the pen, it was more difficult to get them back in – the boys had the major task of actually grabbling them if they didn't run back into the pen on their own. The girls mainly stood at designated points so they couldn't get past us. A special area of the hog pen was built a few feet off the ground and designated for a hog being "fatted" for slaughter.

Chapter 3:

Cultivation – The Land We Love

Spring ushered in a time for planting in the South. Our farm was no exception. Time for clearing the land and making ready for farming was at hand. Seeds, fertilizer, farm equipment, etc. were secured, repaired, readied for the various crops. For most of my childhood, we did not have a tractor so plowing/tilling the crops was done with mules and various types of plows. Rows were mapped out in the field and prepared for planting. Before planting our seeds in those prepared rows, we distributed fertilized from 50-pound bags by hand using smaller buckets as we walked the rows. We then spread the appropriate seeds by hand on those same rows. Crops were raised for sale for income for the household and for providing food for the family to eat. Some of the crops we raised were cotton, cucumbers, corn, sugarcane, sweet potatoes, peas, beans, white potatoes, peanuts, okra, tomatoes, onions, peppers. If it was a Southern staple, I think we raised it.

COTTON

In the South, cotton was king, and especially in Mississippi. Although we didn't have the huge acreage that some farmers had in the Delta part of our State, we had our share. Cotton seeds were dropped by a planter being pulled by a mule for many years and later by a tractor. Fertilizer purchased in 50-pound sacks was poured into buckets to be sown by hand, row by row. When a good stand of plants emerged, the crop was ready to be hoed or chopped to clear unwanted weeds. We had to be taught how to distinguish between the cotton plants and the weeds. Hoes were sharpened by hand to help expedite the weeding process. All the older children were responsible for using a file to sharpen their own hoes every morning and again when we took a lunch break. The younger kids' hoes were sharpened by Daddy. Everybody had their own special hoe. If a new one had to be purchased, everyone wanted it. Fifty-pound bags of ammonia were spread on the crops, and again we children were charged with this task, and it was done by hand with the smaller buckets. We often had to help other farmers with these tasks after completing our own.

Getting new sun hats at the beginning of the planting year was like getting Christmas presents. We were so proud of our hats. They kept the sun from beating down upon our bare heads since we would be in the field many days from sun-up until sun-down. We took care of that hat because we knew we were not getting another one.

When the cotton was ready to be harvested near the end of summer, old cotton sacks were pulled out and new ones purchased if necessary. Once again, we were thrilled to be the one to get the new sack—we didn't know any better! If I remember correctly, the sacks came in three different sizes: 7-foot, 9-foot, and 12 foot. Most people had the 7-foot sack, a few more experienced, stronger pickers had the 9-foot sack, and seldom did our family use a 12-footer. Very young children were blessed with a grass sack (croker sack) recycled from feed or seeds that had been purchased for spring planting. A strap was attached to the grass sack to go around the neck so that it could be pulled. This grass sack was my very first cotton sack. At the age of 5-years-old, I made my cotton-picking debut picked cotton on the row beside my mother. That grass sack gave way to the 7-footer. This was hard work which everyone, boys and girls, along with both parents, was required to do. I remember trying to compete with my siblings to see who could pick more cotton in a day and I always came up short.

As sacks were filled, they were taken to scales for weighing. These scales were attached to the back of the truck into which the sacks of cotton were emptied. Once weighed and emptied, it was back to where we left off on that row. At the end of the day, everyone brought their sacks to the scales to be weighed and emptied. I believe it took several hundred pounds of cotton (1100 pounds or more) to make a bale so this truck which was paneled on all four side, about four feet high, was filled up before it was taken to the cotton gin for sale and processing.

Occasionally, when the truck was not full or ready to go to the gin when we finished the day's work, we would climb aboard and play on the cotton, bouncing and throwing cotton at each other to our heart's content. Rarely did we get to go with daddy to the cotton gin. When we did, we found the truck pulled under this huge vacuum-type pipe that was used to suction all the cotton from the truck. I understood that at the gin the cotton and seeds were separated yielding a bale of cotton weighing around 400 pounds.

Not only were we required to pick cotton on our own farm, but we were also "hired out" to help my uncle, other family members, and neighbors. Every year we would tell our daddy that we did not want to pick for others, but every year we ended up doing it again. Payment was made according to the number of pounds picked the entire day. Since I could never pick that much, needless-to-say I did not earn much money.

Back then, farmers raised huge crops so it was not unusual for one farmer to have 20, 30, even 50 acres of cotton on the large farms. Some years the cotton plants/stalks were very short and you literally had to get on your knees to pick the cotton from the bolls. Some years, the plants/stalks were very tall. I remember one year my uncle's cotton stalks grew to about 8 feet tall and were filled with huge worms. Since I was afraid of worms at that time, I was traumatized having to reach through the leaves to reach in and pull the cotton out of the bolls. I think I did more crying than cotton-picking that day and I know my sack didn't get full. Sometimes the taller stalks (not those with the worms) provided shade from the abusive heat from the sun. As a result, some cotton pickers were caught napping on their sacks. What a blessing it was when the clouds came over the sun and lessened the burning heat. We were thrilled when that happened.

When we picked cotton for others, we would either take our lunch for the day or someone would go to town to purchase something to eat. Water was brought in and provided intermittently during the day. There was one bucket of water and one cup for everybody to drink from. If we were in our field, a tall, round cooler called "a mule" was filled with ice and water and was taken to the field where we drank from it as we got thirsty. Generally, the lunch was a bologna sandwich with Kool-Aid or some type of punch. Again, someone went to the house and prepared the sandwiches and punch and brought it back to the field. Our meal was sometimes prepared and eaten under the nearest/biggest shade tree. After a quick meal and a short break, sometimes stretching out on that cotton sack, it was back to the field. Generally, cotton picking is done when most of the bolls are open and full. A second and occasionally third picking is done when the rest of the bolls become open and full. That final picking was called "scrapping" because there usually was not that much left. Nobody really liked scrapping, especially in the fields of others, because there was not a lot of cotton left and you had to cover the same acreage and the yield (and thus your payment for the day) was not much.

Since cotton harvesting was done in the fall, this was one of those farm tasks that we had to miss school or leave school at noon to take care of. Nobody wanted to be seen in the cotton field when the bus came by in the afternoon after school ended, so we lay on our cotton sacks in the ditch between the rows until the school bus passed.

CUCUMBERS

Raising cucumbers was and is a horse of a different color. These plants grow on the ground, with vines spreading completely across the rows. With bent backs, these vines had to be moved so we could see and pick the cucumbers. This wonderful (haha) job took place every other day – or every day if we didn't get over the entire crop in one day. Most of the time we could get through picking before noon because we hit the field as soon as we could see the cucumbers under the vines. However, I do remember those days when we didn't come out of the field until after lunch (enjoying lunch in the field under the tree) trying to cover the whole crop in one day. Talk about back-bending, all day long. This was it!!! Some of my siblings had homemade knee pads to just crawl along when their back couldn't take it. Every picker had his or her own bucket. Adults generally had a five-gallon bucket. Once that bucket was full, the cucumbers were poured into a grass sack placed at the end of the rows until it was full. Then, on to the next sack. A day's picking could yield 10, 20, or more sacks of cucumbers, depending on the acreage and how much they produced. Cucumbers could not be left on the vine long. If not picked every other day, they would become too big and then become hard. Unless you wore gloves, these "green boys" left your hand badly stained – and it took some scrubbing, even with a knife sometime, to scrape the stains/residue off. The smaller cucumber garnered the highest pay, while the larger one brought less money. When they got too big, they were pulled from the vine and tossed to the side because they were not worth taking to the cucumber vat/sale. Some of these were harvested for personal use, eating and making pickles for the family. Madear would soak the cucumbers in a salt and alum solution I believe for a week or two before transferring them to another solution (not sure of the full process) of vinegar and spices before canning them for the family's use later. I never learned how to preserve pickles.

Occasionally Daddy would treat us by allowing us to ride on top of the sacks on the back of the truck to take the cucumbers to the vat for sale. There the cucumbers were sorted by size for various uses. When we were allowed to go, we each got a nickel and got a chance to go to the local grocer and pick out a snack to spend that nickel on. We were thrilled to give the grocer our money because of the treat we were gonna get. I remember the white merchant would not take money from our hands and would not touch our hands if he had to return change to us. Instead, the money was thrown on the counter for us to pick up. Thank God for childhood innocence - we didn't understand how we were being discriminated against because it was being done that way all around us. It's amazing how those trips, despite the sordid treatment, bring back fond memories!!!

CORN

Another Southern staple we raised was corn. This was one of the crops that did not require the high maintenance some others did. Dry corn kernel seeds were dropped by hand in rows opened by the middle-buster plow pulled behind the mule. When the plants grew, hair-like tassels appeared, followed by ears of corn. When the corn matured, we enjoyed fresh corn on the cob, fried corn, etc. When the corn was dry, we harvested the crop by walking along each row, pulling the ears from the stalks, and strategically placing them in big piles throughout the corn patch. After the corn was piled up, the truck was brought into the field, and we picked it up and loaded it onto the truck for transfer to the crib where it was stored for the winter. Some dry corn was often taken to the mill to be ground into cornmeal for the family's cornbread. At some point, I remember we had our own grinder for removing dry corn from the cob. The corn was then taken to the "grist" mill to be ground into cornmeal. The dry corn was also used to feed the animals (cows, mules, and hogs) over the winter months.

SWEET POTATOES

A favorite Southern staple we raised that did not require constant attention but could require a lot of manpower especially at harvest time was sweet potatoes. We planted our potatoes using a stick to bore holes into the rows a few feet apart, placing the potato stems/plants/ roots in the holes, and surrounding the plant with dirt. This was very time-consuming, and it could do a number on your back if you had to do it all day. I remember Uncle Barney had many acres of sweet potatoes and purchased a piece of farm equipment pulled by the tractor that had two seats, one on each side of a bin. Individuals riding in these two seats took turns dropping the plants into the bin, and fertilizer was automatically dispensed at the same time I believe, as the plants were pressed into the ground. This machine punched the hole and planted the potato stem/root in one step. Since he had a large acreage of sweet potatoes, this was especially helpful as we were often "loaned-out" to help with the planting. Our payment for helping was bartered lunches in the school cafeteria which I'll discuss later. Sweet potatoes grow underground which meant the harvesting process was hard. Plows, whether behind a mule or with a tractor, open the rows up exposing the sweet potatoes that had to be picked up by hand. This was a dirty job. We were given a basket and charged with picking up all the exposed potatoes from the dirt. When our baskets were full, they were dumped into a truck that was in the field. The potatoes were later transferred to a special house for storage and to prevent spoilage. The potato house was a dark, highly insulated, cool place with no windows that had a hallway down the middle. There were large upper and lower bins, sectioned off for some reason, on each side of the hallway where potatoes were placed and covered with straw and saw dust I believe. The door to that house was extremely heavy. There was a light in the hallway that could be turned on when entering and the door was left open when we had to go inside so that we would have adequate lighting. I hated having to go into the "tater" house to get potatoes because it was very scary to me – claustrophobic, if you like.

These potatoes lasted throughout the winter months, providing food for the families as well as a huge food supply for some of the animals. The potatoes my parents raised were placed in a "bank" where they were stored for the winter. This bank was a huge mound of dirt with an opening/door to access the potatoes. I remember many days having to go to the bank, reaching through that dirt and pine straw, searching for potatoes for baking or roasting in the wood heater and later in the oven of our gas stove. Add a little butter or oleo and some sugar and you have a delicacy that can't be compared. Sweet potatoes were very popular during my growing up years and they continue to be a Southern favorite. While potato pones, casseroles, cakes, and other uses are good, nothing compares to the sweet potato pie.

PEANUTS

With the acquisition of the tractor, another crop that was made easier to raise was peanuts. While the planting of the peanuts was not that bad, the harvesting was tough. Picking peanuts off the vine and picking those out of the dirt that had been dislodged from the vine was hard on the body. Rather than waiting for the mule and plow to open the rows and uncover the peanuts, the tractor could pull the plants from the ground quickly, thus allowing us to gather the vines together more expeditiously and load them on a truck as we picked up those peanuts left on the ground. Depending on the size of the peanut patch and the yield, sometimes this whole process of pull-up, pick-off was done in the field. Otherwise, the vines were loaded on a truck and brought to the home where there was a peanut-picking party under the big oak tree in front of the family home. Once the peanuts were pulled from the vine, they were washed and laid out to dry. While the peanuts were green, we enjoyed boiled peanuts for many days.   I must admit I ate my share of raw peanuts and they were good, and I didn't get sick. When they were physically dry, they were place in croker (grass) sacks, hung from the rafters, and stored in the smoke house or crib to completely dry out. Those dry peanuts were roasted and enjoyed while we sat around the fire during the winter months. A special treat was making peanut brittle and chowing down on it on a Saturday night.

SUGAR CANE

Any girl raised in the south will tell you there is nothing like hot biscuits with homemade molasses (sugarcane syrup). Syrup or molasses making was a community affair as it took several people to perform the tasks. The nearest cane mill to us belonged to my Uncle Barney. Many neighbors, as well as others in the community, came to his mill at harvest time to make their syrup. Often several farmers would gather their annual harvest, schedule a time to bring it to the mill, and wait their turn as others in line ahead of them helped with the actual molasses-making process for their cane. These farmers often agreed to help with the syrup-making and payment was made to the mill owner in the form of a percentage of or number of gallons of syrup per farmer/crop.   It sometimes took several days to get everybody's syrup made. From planting to pouring into the can, the process of making syrup or molasses was a tough one. Stalks of sugar cane that had been banked (seed cane stored in the ground over the winter and saved for planting) were dug up and planted for the current year's crop. Stalks were placed end-to-end in open rows and buried. The plants grew over the summer. In the fall, when the crop was ready for harvesting, we knew it was time to remove the tops and the dry leaves and blades from the stalks, better known as "stripping cane". The sugarcane blades were very sharp and could cut into your skin, so we had to make sure we wore long sleeves and were completely covered.

Some of the stalks of sugar cane grew to 6-15 feet. A large knife was used to cut the tops off the stalks and cut the stalks down after a long handle cane-stripper was used to strip the leaves/blades from the stalk.   The cane-stripper was a long, wooden slat with two metal, knife-type blades with curved hooks on the end attached to the slat. Once stripped and cut down, the stalks of cane were placed between the rows in large piles where they were later picked up and taken to the cane mill for processing.

Once the cane reached the mill, a few stalks at a time were then fed through a machine with rollers used to squeeze the juice out. In the early years, this machine with multiple gears and a long, wide belt was powered by a mule going around in circles. Later a tractor was used to power this machine, but the same process was followed. Shredded stalks were stacked in a pile not far from the machine. At least two to three people were constantly feeding the machine and removing the shredded stalks and tossing them into a pile with a rake. The juice was pressed into a large tub with a croker (burlap) grass sack on top for straining or filtering the juice of impurities or pieces of cane. The juice was then allowed to flow through pipes into a large vat in the cane mill where the cooking process was done.

The cooking vat was a very thick iron pan, about 30-50 feet long, with side about a foot high. Spigots were attached to allow the juice to flow at the top end of the vat and spigots were attached to the bottom end where the readied syrup was funneled into metal cans. The cooking vat was about 4 feet off the ground and sat atop a tunnel-shaped fire-pit made of iron and banked in clay that had been hardened/baked over iron supports. Lots of wood was needed for processing so it was gathered before the syrup making began. Before the juice was run into the vat, lots of wood, the length of trees, was placed under the vat to cook the juice. A fire was made and had to be maintained all day to get and keep the juice at a certain temperature. A long metal fire stoker-poker was used to keep the fire-pit (oven) hot by adding more wood as needed.

During the cooking process, long shovels and paddles were used to stir the juice. Once it began to boil, they were used to skim the surface to remove foam and any small pieces of cane or impurities that floated to the surface. The juice was moved along the pan as it cooked and had to reach and remain at a rolling boil for a long time before it reached syrup density/thickness and could be canned. New juice coming into the top of the vat pushed the other juice along until it all reached the desired consistency or scalding and was ready to fill the syrup cans. New syrup cans often had to be purchased yearly. After the syrup was canned and the task for the day was complete, the wood remaining under the pan was pulled away and the pan cleaned. The process started again the next day until everybody's syrup was made. Madear was very good at making syrup and was almost always called to help during the entire syrup-making process.

A small amount of the sugar cane was not processed but was left to be enjoyed by individuals, adults and children alike, who peeled and chewed the stalk to get the juice from it. In addition, some of the juice was not cooked but left for drinking by those who enjoyed a cold glass of cane juice. A lot of farmers raised sugarcane for the purpose of making syrup to sell and there were lots of people waiting to purchase it.

PEAS/BEANS/OKRA/TOMATOES/ETC.

Some people called them gardens, but we called them fields because of the acreage of the peas, beans, okra, onions, tomatoes, etc. A good bit of farmland was utilized for growing vegetables. Most of the families in our area raised their own vegetable crops. Some of it was for feeding their families but the larger farms raised these crops to sell, and they provided a good source of income for them. Peas and beans were measured by the peck and bushel. These plants grow in bushes, some with climbing vines. They are harvested when the pods containing the peas and beans are full or mature. If the vines or bushes grew too tall, we had to attach stakes beside them to keep them from falling on the ground. Large pails or small sacks were used in picking these veggies. They were then brought from the field and the shelling process began for those peas and beans retained for family consumption. Not everybody could pick peas and beans because you had to be able to determine which ones were ready and which ones needed to stay on the vine and grow further. You did not want to pull a lot of those not ready because that would reduce your yield as these would not have time to grow. However, everyone could join in on the shelling party. Bowls were filled and the shelling began. The peas were shelled, washed several times, cooked, and eaten or blanched for canning. While shelling, some unlucky children were known to get peas stuck in their noses and require help getting them out. Somehow, some even had peas land in their ears and in one case the pea began to sprout and had to be removed by a doctor.

Okra is a great Southern staple. It is one of those vegetables that either you really love it, or you really hate it. Fried okra is a big favorite of many. I enjoy it boiled, fried, in gumbo, etc. I could eat it almost every day. One of my sisters hated it. She said the thought of eating something that look and feel that slimy was disgusting.

Okra plants (or seeds) were spaced about a foot apart so they would have plenty of room to grow. Looking like flowers as they begin to grow, the okra plants grow into stalks. Rows had to be cleared (hoed) to prevent unwanted grass and weeds. The plants grew into stalks which were 4-5 feet in height. When the pods appeared, they had to be picked within a day or two while they were still soft and could be eaten. When left on the stalk longer, the pods became hard and was not usable for consumption. They then had to be tossed, used for feeding animals, or allowed to dry for seed for the next year's crop. The smaller the pods, the better. Some type of covering was needed for your hand when gathering okra (pulling by hand or cutting with a knife) because the plants have tiny spines that would irritate (scratch and sting) your skin and cause excessive itching. We used gloves when we had them or old socks if we didn't have gloves. It was always important to wear long sleeves when gathering okra. Once the readied pods were pulled, they continued flowering/blooming and more pods appeared. Gathering had to be done almost every other day to get the best yield from your crop. Okra can be stored in the freezer either cooked or blanched; I believe we blanched ours.

Everybody enjoyed a good tomato. Some people used seeds and some used seedling plants to start their crop. Since there are so many varieties of tomatoes, the size of the plant and the size of the actual tomato could vary. When the tomato plants started to grow, we had to place sticks (stakes) beside them to keep them from falling over and the tomatoes growing on the ground. Tomatoes were picked when they were green and when they were ripe. We grew them for personal consumption -- eating and for canning -- but some farmers grew them for marketing. Fried green tomatoes were and still are considered a Southern delicacy. And, maybe not as popular, but just as good, is tomato gravy made with ripe tomatoes and a flour roux. Our tomatoes were cut, blanched, and canned for use during the winter months as well. A tomato-based soup in the winter months went a long way for a large family and came in quite handy for a sick child or adult.

We didn't have a pecan tree, but my uncle did and sometimes there were "volunteer" trees that grew in the woods from seeds probably taken there by squirrels or other animals. Regardless of where we got them, we enjoyed eating pecans in the pies and other cooked goodies as well as eating them straight from the tree. We had hickory trees on our farm that yielded nuts. We gathered these nuts and enjoyed them over the winter months. These nuts were large oval nuts that had a shell that is very thick and hard to crack. We often used a hammer or brick to crack them open. We didn't have to compete with the squirrels for the fruit from this nut.

FRUITS AND BERRIES

Living in the country, we had access to lots of fresh fruits and berries. Many of the berries grew wild and were there for whoever desired to gather them. Picking berries was a fun time to me because we could laugh and talk and explore the woods as we did this job. This was a group activity, and we almost always had a crowd when we set out early in the morning to gather berries. With our buckets in hand, we raced to the bushes with the biggest blueberries and the vines with the largest blackberries. Once our buckets were full, and we had eaten all we wanted from the bushes, we took the berries home where they were washed before preparing for canning, for making cobblers, pies, or for eating raw.

Peaches, pears, and apples were pulled from trees grown on the farm during their harvest season. As they ripened, some fell from the tree and could be picked up from the ground. Others were picked from branches within our reach. For those we could not reach, a long stick or fishing pole was used to knock them down. We ate many of them, cooked with some, and canned the rest. The activities on canning day included washing, peeling, and cutting the fruit off the core. The fruit was then ready to be cooked. Mason jars were washed and heated in preparation for the hot fruit that would be poured into them. We canned a lot of fruits and vegetables. Most of our canning was in quart jars. When we acquired a deep freezer, fresh fruit was then stored in plastic bags in the freezer as well as in jars.

Madear and the girls were charged with the task of canning vegetables. Those Mason jars and lids were heated in boiling water while the peas/beans were slightly cooked or "blanched" in a large pot. Once they reached a boil, they were poured into the jars with some of the liquid they were boiled in, and the jars were sealed. These jars were placed upside down on a towel and usually left that way overnight to ensure proper sealing was attained. The process of blanching vegetables that were stored in the deep freezer was the same. One the boiling point was achieved, these vegetables were drained of liquid and spread out on a towel or sheet to absorb the excess water and cool. This was necessary before they could be placed in plastic bags, dated, and stored in the freezer.

Chapter 4:

Moving Into The Electronic World

RADIO/TELEVISION/TELEPHONE

For many of my elementary school years, we did not have a television. The radio was our best friend. Not only did we get music, preaching, and the news, but back then several shows aired over the radio. One of the favorites in our house was The Green Hornet. I remember Sunday evenings was a time everybody gathered around the radio because nobody wanted to miss the show. The half-hour radio program "The World Tomorrow" with Herbert W. Armstrong was one of Madear's favorites and thus a regular airing at our house. We listened to lots of gospel music.

Reception of radio stations in our area was limited. We had a few country stations, but we were able to access one station broadcasting out of Tennessee that played rock and roll and blues music. I clearly remember the disc jockey called "John R" came on with the saying, "Hey John R man, what you gonna do? Come on John R man and play some rhythm and blues." From the sound of his voice, I assumed he was a Black guy. Not until I was an adult did I find out that he was not Black, but White John Richbourg on WLAC. I understand he had other shows entrances, but this is the way I remember him starting his broadcast.

Television – my, my, my! When I was a young child, we did not have a television. They were around, we just didn't have one. Lucky for us, our grandfather (paw-paw Steve, he's a whole other story) allowed us to come to his house to watch tv. He lived a few houses away, that's half a country mile, from us. Since we worked in the field during the day, we only got to watch tv at night in the summer or the weekend. So, with a lighted pine torch (lighted knot), a group of us struck out on the gravel road headed to paw-paw's house. Our tv time was limited but my brother Robert Earl and paw-paw could watch late into the night and then he was left to come home late at night by himself. Back in those days, the television stations went off the air at midnight with the singing of the National Anthem. This brother was often reprimanded by my parents because of those late-night stays. He never considered the dangers, and there were lots of wild animals roaming in those days.

I remember THE DAY we finally got a television of our own. It was during cucumber-picking season. I don't know if daddy had taken cucumbers to the vat and got paid and then went and purchased the tv or what, but I do know when he returned, he had a tv. Of course, we all had to come out of the cucumber patch, which was right by the house, to christen that thang. And, of course, we all had to go back to the cucumber patch and finish picking for that day. That same brother who got in trouble for the late-night tv viewing at pawpaw's had the same problem with our tv. I remember he would turn the volume down very low so nobody would know he was still up watching tv. Years later, when many of us had left home and he had his own private room, he got his personal tv and enjoyed it to his contentment.

Telephones didn't reach our part of the country until I was in middle or high school. Even then, we shared a "party-line" with another phone subscriber. I don't remember being allowed to use the phone till my later teenage years. One humorous thing that comes to mind about that time was a neighbor who also had a party-line phone. She was fearful of the phone and when she called someone, she would not say anything, waiting for the person she called to say hello so she could recognize the voice of the person she thought she was calling. Once she dialed a wrong number and, as usual, waited for the person she called to say something. She didn't recognize the voice, so she didn't say anything but just held the phone. Well, after saying hello a few times, the guy on the other end of the call, tired of not getting a response made the following statement: "Ass speak, your mouth won't," to which she quickly hung up the phone.

Chapter 5:

Clothes/Shoes

Growing up in the South in a large family meant that there weren't a lot of new clothes. Hand-me-downs from older siblings was the way of life. Homemade clothes were worn by most folks, especially the females of the family. Madear made some clothes for us. One of my dad's sisters, Aunt Mary who we call Aunt Can, had no children and would make dresses for us which we really didn't like but had to wear anyway. Not having children, she viewed clothes from her age/point of view, but they appeared as long, grandma dresses to us and to our peers.

Once a month, I believe, my parents went to a monthly sale at what I call a precursor of the Dirt Cheap Store of today that we called "The Lunky". This sale was held at the Piney Woods Country Life School and another sale was held at a location in Simpson County. There they secured clothes for us. We were thrilled to see what goodies they found for us. Another help in the clothing department was an annual box from Chicago from our grandmother, Maw Maw Missouri. Again, we were thrilled to tear into the box to discover what goodies she had sent to us.

We each had a pair of school shoes and later a pair of church shoes. New shoes were few and far between. Our shoes ranged from the black and white oxfords which we referred to "hello buckles" to hush puppies. One year, my hush puppies were so worn that there was a hole in the bottom where I had to put a piece of cardboard so I could continue wearing them. Wet hush puppies were a drag; they faded on your socks. As we got older, we did get some store-bought clothes. Even though we didn't have a lot of new clothes, my mama insisted that we wear cleaned and ironed clothes and that we kept our bodies clean – personal hygiene was a must.

Chapter 6:

Trip Down Memory Lane (Part 2)

It was fun making quilts for the family and seeing what our new creative projects looked like. We began the process by sewing left-over pieces of cloth (from those homemade clothes) together to make a top for the quilt. Generally, a solid piece of material used as the bottom of the quilt was attached to a quilting frame. This frame was made of light-weight wood rails about 1x1 inches and had clamps to pin the quilt on. The rails had four joining pieces with holes drilled in them so the frame could be expanded to accommodate up to a king size bed and rolled up as the quilt was completed. Batting (cotton without seeds) was spread between the bottom and top pieces of cloth. Once a portion of the quilt had been completed, the railing was rolled up toward the center. This was done until the quilt was finished. Once finished, the quilt was removed from the frame and the overlapping bottom of the quilt was pulled over the top and stitched in place to complete the quilt. The frame was large and it took up most of the space in the family room and it could take more than one day to complete a quilt. When it was not being worked on, and while it was in the making, the frame which was attached by ropes/strings on all four corners, was pulled up to the ceiling so you could walk under it. With several people working around the quilt frame, it proved a good time to tell stories and to laugh a lot. Several quilts were made each year and provided comfort and can I say a touch of beauty to each bed.

Most children raised in the South, not just girls, ate their share of dirt. And not just any ole dirt. Clay dirt! We didn't eat it like a meal, but just an occasional snack. Not all dirt was good to eat or clean, so we removed the upper layer of dirt and had a ball enjoying that red clay dirt underneath. I tried to encourage a cousin/classmate to indulge but she didn't find it as appealing as we did.

As a young girl, we often didn't have the luxury of a store-bought doll – heck, any store-bought toys. We used bricks for our doll babies. We would clothe them and feed them with a play baby bottle that had once held concentrated punch. Our playhouses were on the ground in the yard where it had been scraped clean and we even sectioned off rooms within the playhouse. We learned to plait or braid hair using grass.

Cartoon characters are not the only ones who enjoyed playing in the mud after a big rain. As children, we had a lot of fun playing in the muddy ditches after a big rain not knowing what could be lurking in there. Surprisingly nobody was ever bitten by a snake or other rodent or reptile even though there were plenty of them around.

Contrary to popular belief, not all Southerners have a mouth full of rotten teeth or are missing all of them. Necessity truly is the mother of invention. I have never had to use one, but as a small child I saw people use the tool made from a twig from a tree as a toothbrush. These sticks were chewed until one end was frayed. That frayed end was then used to brush against the teeth to prevent tooth decay and gum disease. Some people even put baking soda on the frayed end for extra protection and cleaning. The twig was usually from a birch or sweetgum tree I believe.

Anywhere you went in the South, among all races, you could find an adventurous child not old enough to smoke cigarettes, as well as the casual adult user, finding delight in rolling up those homemade cigarettes made from "rabbit tobacco" plants that grow wild. Robert Earl was our adventurous one. They say Native Americans used rabbit tobacco and that it was not addictive. He sure liked it a lot – I think he got addicted. He later tried to sneak and smoke real cigarettes.

Thank God nobody in my immediate family indulged in "snuff dipping" but several relatives were dippers, including pawpaw's third wife. The smell of it always made me nauseated but the snuff lovers could put a small amount between their bottom lip and lower teeth and, I guess, enjoy the juice it provided. Likewise, we had no tobacco chewers in the immediate family, so we didn't have to deal with the wads of chewed tobacco, or the brown spit left everywhere.

Candies and store-bought cookies were real treats. A favorite among us all was the stage plank, a ginger cookie with hard pink glazed frosting. Other favorites included moon pies and big boy vanilla cookies. Those were the biggest sandwich cookies and there were three rows of them. Yummy!! And, you could get a whole bag for only $1.00. As good as they were, nothing compared to my mama's molasses cakes or my auntie's tea cakes. Oh, to enjoy one of those now.

Some Southern food favorites were hoecakes (fried cornbread cooked on top of the stove) and collard greens, flapjack (cake-type pancake) and syrups. Sometimes those syrups were the sugarcane molasses and sometimes they were syrup made on top of the stove by boiling sugar and water together until it thickened.

Learning to cook was something we all were encouraged to do. I made my first cake, not from cake mix but from scratch, at the tender age of 12-years old — and it was good too. We enjoyed homemade pies made with fruit (apples, peaches, pears) we picked and cobblers with the berries we picked. As hard as I tried, I was never able to master Madear's gift of making fluffy biscuits.

Every country boy was taught to hunt and fish. As far back as I can remember, my daddy loved hunting and fishing. While he never did it on a large scale, he loved to indulge whenever he had a spare moment. Almost everybody loved to fish. In my early years, we did not have a pond of our own so we would fish at my uncle's pond, a local stream, in the nearby creek, and the river. When we got our own pond and it was stocked with fish, most of us chose to stay close to home. We made our fishing poles with bamboo cane that grew in the woods behind our house and near the pond. Daddy brought hooks, line, and sinkers that we attached to the poles. Most of the time, we used earthworms we dug or crickets for fish bait. Occasionally daddy would purchase some bait or we would use small pieces of salt-pork (fat back) for bait. When we became teenagers and earned money working for other farmers or when we reached adulthood, we upgrade to fishing rods.

A certain time of year, I believe it was May or June, the men in the community and sometimes older boys would go to the river at night with spear-type "gigs" with hooks to catch redhorse fish from the river. These large fishes would weigh 8-10 pounds or more and were about 1-2 feet long. Lots of good eating.

Not as often as the rabbit and squirrel hunting, daddy would occasionally hunt and kill wild turkeys or geese. While the hunting and catching of the game was fun, the cleaning and prep-work for cooking and/or freezing was not a pleasant task. It was always a team effort to skin a rabbit or squirrel and I hated to try to get the scales off the fishes we caught.

A tradition in the South that showed respect regardless of race was that of vehicles pulling to the side of the road when they met a funeral procession. However, there were some customs or traditions associated with death that many people have never heard about, even though some happened during my lifetime. When I mentioned one recently, the younger people in the room thought I was making it up or had just lost my mind. Years ago, the body of a deceased family member was brought to the family home for the visitation or wake and people came to the house for the viewing. Thereafter, the body remained in the family home overnight and up until time for the funeral the following day. Thankfully, when I mentioned it, there was one person in the group who has personally witnessed this when her grandmother and great-grandmother died, and they were kept in the home overnight before the funeral the next day.

Farmers back then did not have grave digging equipment. Because of that, when someone in the community or church died, the relatives of the deceased and other men in the community came together to dig the grave by hand with picks and shovels. The request was sent around for men/boys to help dig a grave.   I remember my daddy and my brothers talking about and coming home muddy after standing in the freshly dug graves.

As an adult, I would later witness the passing of one of the mothers of our church during Sunday service. A very lively person, she suffered a heart attack and was not able to be revived. One of the sisters in the church noticed she was not moving and didn't know if she was asleep or not feeling well so she went to her pew to check on her and discovered that she was unresponsive. Paramedics were called and resuscitation efforts began, but they were unable to revive her. She had passed.

Store bought toys and things like bicycles were not a part of our livelihood. I remember once my uncle bought a new bike for my oldest brother who lived with him and his wife next door to us. He found a used bike that he brought to us that the other 12 children that lived in our house had to share. A lot of things that we now look back on with wonderment and disdain, but at the time we were thrilled to have a bike, even if we didn't get to ride often because we had to take turns. Of course, under the wear and tear of several children, it did not last very long.

I thank God for my mama, Madear. I'll have lots more to say about her elsewhere in the book. She never set foot in a medical school but even with her limited education, she knew enough home remedies to handle medical conditions that we encountered over the years. She was so good that other relatives and neighbors would call upon her when they had health problems.

I am still intrigued by the wisdom that our elders demonstrated. Many times, it was in the form of old "sayings". One of our elderly, grandmotherly neighbors had a word for people when they were not aware of something or did not fully understand the meaning of something. She let them know that "there was enough they did not know to make a whole 'nother world with a basement."

They used metaphors to make you use your brain. When passing the cemetery, they would ask what we thought was a guessing question of "How many dead people were in that cemetery?" While we fumbled around trying to give an educated guess, they would answer the question letting us know that "that everybody in the cemetery is dead." Another example was that of announcing that somebody "had been run over by the train," not realizing that the person had only driven under the viaduct when the train was passing on the track overhead. Not sure of the accuracy, but intrigued by it anyway, were sayings like "when it was raining and the sun was shining, the devil was beating his wife" and "if a snapping turtle bit you, it would hold on and not let you go until it thundered."

Chapter 7:

Education

Most children remember their first day of school. So do I! My classroom was housed in an old wooden white building at the back of the school campus.   That day was memorable not just because it was my first day of school, but because we (my oldest sister, Stella, who was charged with making sure I got on the bus and I) missed the bus returning home. The assistant school principal, Mr. Clayton, agreed to drop us off at home on his way to his house.   Back then, we rode a "big" bus but for some reason, not sure if school population shift, overcrowding, or whatever, we were later relegated to another style of transportation.

You've heard of the proverbial "short bus." Well, later we rode a short bus. This had nothing to do with our intellectual abilities but because our bus route and one other route located on the opposite side of the school did not have enough students for a full-size passenger bus. This short bus ran the two routes, both in the morning and in the afternoon. Since the bus driver lived on our side of the school, we were picked up first and dropped off at the school well ahead of the general student population. The bus then made the second route in time to get students on the other route to school before the first bell rang. Over the years, we learned to play baseball and do other fun things outside before the other students arrived. I'm not sure what we smelled like after playing that early in the morning, but we were ready to learn when the others arrived. For the return trip, the second group went home first at the dismissal bell, and we waited till the bus came back to campus to pick us up for our return trip home.

Later on, our route was combined with another route on our side of the school, and we advanced to the "big" bus again. I remember we had two separate drivers. One was a cousin and family friend who was loved by all the children. The other was not liked very well by the children because he was constantly threatening to report/reporting students to the principal's office for very minor issues, such as talking on the bus. Since this was a combined route, we were packed in there pretty tightly. Generally there were three students per seat and some of the older students from the prior route did not want to share their seats. I remember having to sit with an older male student (SCG) because he would not let a lot of people sit with him, but he would not let me pass his seat. I was always afraid of him. I was glad when he graduated.

Although our attendance center was not huge, my class had the largest number of students per grade during our elementary years. There were three different sections of our grade/class, so I didn't really get to know some of my classmates until we reached middle school. I was never a big fan of school, but I loved seeing my friends and classmates every day. I knew I had to do my very best academically, so I never made an "F" during my school years. I was always an "A", and occasionally a "A-B" student. I hated homework especially when I did not understand something. My parents had so many children to help with homework, after a day of cooking, cleaning, and working in the fields, that they could not spend a lot of time with each child. This motivated me to search for answers and never give up or settle for anything less than good – not perfect – but good. My mama always reminded us of the saying, "If a task is once begun, never leave it till it's done, be the labor great or small, do it well or not at all."

In these days when children are afforded free and reduced lunches and choose not to take advantage of them, I am reminded that this was not an option during my school years. For many years, we prepared and took our lunch to school every day. I remember the years when our lunch consisted of two peanut butter-saltine cracker sandwiches per child and three pennies to purchase a carton of milk from the cafeteria to wash it down. The milk later went up to a nickel for two cartons, then inflation hit, and it went up to a nickel for one carton. Each morning one of the older siblings prepared the peanut butter-cracker sandwiches for the group and put them in one big brown paper bag to take to school. In those days, everybody went to lunch at the same time so we would meet the sibling in charge of distributing the lunch to get our two sandwiches at lunchtime. Strangely, I don't remember being hungry even though many of my friends and classmates were eating a full meal in the cafeteria.

For a short period of time during the fall, we ate in the cafeteria. Vaguely, I was thinking it was just for the Thanksgiving Lunch, but my sister reminded me it was not just one day but for a longer period of time. Our cafeteria lunch was a trade-off between my uncle and the school for sweet potatoes he provided for the school cafeteria. We helped harvest these sweet potatoes and this was our payment.

The school I attended for the first 11 years was a grades 1-12 attendance center; kindergarten was not around in those days. Our principal (Mr. Lovell Gray) was a strong, strict disciplinarian who didn't mind correcting any student, but he was a good teacher and encouraged the students to be the best they could be. Weekly chapel services were held with speakers and/or different classes providing the entertainment/program. Mr. Gray shared many encouraging words from educational to personal hygiene. During EVERY chapel program, he admonished the students to "wash down to possible, wash up to possible, and by all means, don't forget to wash possible." When classes were charged with the weekly chapel program, students were required to learn and deliver speeches, perform skits, display talents, etc. That exposure helped many students develop self-confidence and instill leadership characteristics that set the foundation for the men and women that they are today.

A frequent chapel speaker and a very fond memory was that of Rev. John Perkins and the Voice of Calvary Ministry. They helped instill a spiritual foundation that remains with many former students today. I remember we were challenged to learn Bible verses, and once a specific number of verses were learned, students were eligible to attend a week-long camp during the summer months. The year I finally achieved that goal, the facility burned down before time for the camp to meet and I was very disappointed that I couldn't go.

Our school, and especially the hallways, was always immaculate. I think the principal had a bit of OCD. Classes were charged with keeping their home rooms clean and every week a different class/grade was charged with helping the janitor by cleaning the grounds around the school. When we got a new gym, the floors were kept waxed and clean enough to eat off. After fifty years, the floor in that gym still looks good!

Unlike many of the children today, our school did not have lockers for the students to store their books/ notebooks/etc. between classes so we carried around those 5, 6, or 7 books all day, every day. Seldom, if ever did we get new books at our school. Our books were passed down to us after being used at the white schools in our county for several years. Even so, we were encouraged to be good stewards of the books we had and were charged a fine at the end of the year if a book got damaged or was lost. I remember cutting and using brown paper bags to make covers for my books so that they would not get damaged or dirty. Sometimes books had no backs or had several pages missing at the beginning and/or ending. Book bags were not popular back then, so we had a stack of books, along with a loose-leaf binder, to lug to and from school daily. Thankfully, by the time I started schools, we were being picked up by the bus in front of our house. Several of my older siblings had to walk approximately one country mile to the bus stop in the morning and back to the house in the afternoon.

School supplies were precious commodities. We each got a pencil and several sheets of filler paper from a large pack and knew to make the most of it because we didn't get it often. In other words, you better keep up with your pencil and not mess up that paper. Some students were blessed to have lots of paper and would share with us sometimes, but we never had that spare to share.

I had several influential teachers who invested in me. From the first-grade teacher Miss McIntosh, to my math teacher and Assistant Principal Mr. Robert Clayton, a preacher who was the epitome of a properly dressed black man and who expected students to give it their best. If you took his class after one of your siblings had been in his class, get ready to do as well as or better than your sibling because comparison would be made. If one of his students seemed arrogant in any way, he was quick to let them know when they were "getting the big head." His mild mannerism sometimes led students to think he would not punish them. Not so. He had some yardsticks that saw lots of action.

One incident happened in Mr. Clayton's class which remains a mystery to this day with no one admitting being the culprit. After lecturing from the blackboard for a while, he returned to his desk to sit down only to be greeted by a thumb tack in his seat. To this day, many of the students believe the tack fell from material/ decoration hanging above the blackboard or fell from his desk when he got up and I can honestly say I don't remember anyone leaving their seat while he was at the board. After inquiring as to the guilty party and no one coming forth, the entire class was punished --- lined up and given a paddling with that rod of correction if I remember correctly.

My Home Economics teacher, Mrs. Morris, was a tough cookie that took no prisoners. She traveled from the city to our little town to teach and she loved her students. Another stern disciplinarian, you didn't get out of her class if you didn't know how to cook, how to sew, etc., things I wish were being taught in all high schools now.

Sister to Mrs. Morris, Miss Fannie McCall was one of my favorites. The BEST English and literature teacher I ever had. An inspiration to us all, she had a vision and hearing problem and used a magnifying glass to view the board and classwork and wore a hearing aid. She had one of the best handwritings I have ever seen. She sponsored many class plays, assisted many valedictorians with their addresses, served as senior class advisor, served as yearbook advisor, and sponsor of the school paper. We learned and performed many skits and plays while in her class; we learned and recited many poems in front of the class. I still remember most of "Casey at the Bat" and parts of other poems after fifty years.

I'll never forget that fateful morning in Miss McCall's class when we got word that one of our classmates had died. We knew the weather was quite furious that morning, but we had no inkling it had been that bad. A tornado spun during the early morning hours had claimed the life of our classmate, Vaughn, his mother, sister, brother, and family friend. Another sister and uncle were seriously injured. Sadly, the body of his sister was said to have been found in a nearby tree. The uncle and surviving sister both lost limbs. It was a very somber day for all.

My history teachers, Mr. (later Dr.) Haynes, Mr. Smith, Mr. Watts, etc. required that we keep up with current events, even checking to make sure that we knew what was happening in the world, in our nation, and in our state. We learned and recited before the class the names of all 82 counties in our state, every state and capital of the United States, every European country and its capital, Presidents, the current President and his entire cabinet, and much more. They didn't play! I remember being required to watch the news nightly (thank God we had tv by then) and discuss it the next day. We knew what was happening in the world, nation, state, and even locally.

My elementary teachers were super and I'm so thankful they didn't give up on us. Not to brag, but I always came out in the top ranking of whatever class I attempted. Recess was always a fun time for everybody. In the early years, we had a merry-go-round, a jungle-jim/monkey bars, see-saw, and one of the girls' favorite activities was the "jump board." It was always a challenge to see who could jump the highest or who could send the person jumping against them highest in the air. I remember one day we were jumping, and a classmate pushed the board away when the person jumping against me sent me high into the air. When I came down and hit the ground hard, I felt like my stomach had been pushed up into my chest. Thankfully, there was no major injury.

Our parents did not allow a lot of overnight visits to other homes and, needless to say, those who came to stay overnight with us was limited. However, over the years, I was allowed to spend the night with a classmate and some cousins. I spent a school night with classmate Alice Ray and my cousin Agnes. I also spent the night with my first cousin Linda, (child of daddy's sister) and one of my best friends/cousin Joann. Joann always was and continues to be a very humorous and adventurous person. While at their house, someone made a cake, and she was charged with making the frosting for it. The cake tasted good, but the frosting missed the mark. As she was preparing the frosting, she started adding milk to the powdered sugar. I told her to add the milk very slowly, but she didn't think I knew what I was talking about and just poured it in, saying that she would mix it in, and it would be okay. Well, that watery frosting ran all over the place. Hopefully, she learned to trust me after that.

Some of the boys in my family were allowed to participate sports but the girls were not involved in a lot of extracurricular activities. During middle school, I tried my hand at basketball. Although by that time we had a gym at our school that the middle school could use, we played some schools where the game was played on a dirt basketball court. Of course, all these games were held during the school day/hours, and I actually played in a few games.

Since we didn't have money for lunch, we definitely didn't have money to attend games, sock hops, plays, etc. held during the school day. Students like us with limited funds were relegated to the classroom (sometimes combined with another teachers' class to be supervised) while those with money attended those functions. Occasionally a classmate would have extra funds and would pay for one of us to attend something. Depending on the supervising teacher, those of us left behind learned to make the most of our time and had fun.

Our school always had championship teams. By the time I left the attendance center, numerous 6-10-foot-long trophy cases filled with trophies lined the entrance to our school. These awards were earned by the football team, boys' and girls' basketball team, etc. The cheer, "Can't nobody beat the green and gold" resonated in the ears of our rival schools. Of all the schools we played, there was one that was infamous because of the tactics they used on and off the football field or basketball court. If they didn't beat the team "on the field", they would physically beat them up "after the game". Sadly, the year our schools were integrated, and the attendance center downgraded to an elementary school, all those trophies mysteriously disappeared, never to be seen again ---

and no one acknowledged moving them or disclosed their location. Many people feared they were burned/destroyed.

Our school days did include extra activities that were fun events. If I remember correctly, most of these activities took place the last hour of the school day known as activity period. I did not attend a lot of them because I didn't have the money to attend. There were fund-raising sock-hops/dances and once even a kangaroo fight. Our pep-rallies were always fun. May 1 signified May Day at school which was always a festive day. Everybody got excited and had lots of fun as we prepared to wrap the May Pole. Many students with long streaming ribbon or strips of cloth gathered in a huge circle each holding that streamer in hand as they were waiting to repeatedly begin going under, then over the person next to them till the pole was completed wrapped and everybody has reached the pole. A big draw also was the greased-pole which folks tried to climb to win the prize at the top (sometimes a ham or money). For many years, we had a great school band and school homecoming activities were a big deal. Although, I never got to participate in the activities, just watching the decorated floats, the beautiful homecoming queens and their courts, the band, and the majorettes marching was awesome.

Every year, several classes/grades were selected and performed plays. These programs were held at night and families and friends were invited to attend. This was a good motivator in helping build confidence in students and set up many to enhance their leadership skills and go on to become community and business leaders. It also served to enhance a closer relationship between home and school.

My sister, Eva, was valedictorian of her senior class. She was and still is very smart. I remember her writing and practicing her speech at home. She did an excellent presentation. After high school, she enrolled in Piney Wood Country Life School which had a college program at that time. She was the first child in our family to attend college. I don't remember how long she attended but I don't believe she obtained a degree before she decided to leave the state and move to Chicago to work.

Being smart and being poor in school brought its share of bullying. I remember classmates getting mad with me and talking negatively about me because I would not let them see or "copy off" my paper and when I scored higher on tests than everyone else. Since we didn't always have new clothes and shoes as others did, we were sometime pushed back or talked about. I determined at an early age that I would not let this bother me. I had a loving family and a personal relationship with God and faith in His love for me, so I was not swayed – not saying I was not hurt, because I was.   Again, being poor, we did not always have the fancy lotions or toiletries that others may have had. Vaseline and Royal Crown were our body lotions. I remember being teased about having "greasy" legs with statements such as "If a fly lands on her legs, he will get stuck." Even with the bullies, I still had true friends who cared about and supported me.

Since school was not one of my favorite pastimes, I was thrilled when we got out of school for the summer break. Staying in touch with friends and classmates over the summer break was done by mail through the U. S. Postal Service. I remember sending letters for a nickel (5 cent). As soon as I got a letter in the mail, I would turn around and write them back the next day. I had one friend tell me that "you don't have to write back right away." To this day, I still love to send cards/inspirational info to family and friends through snail mail. Sending letters to pen-pals was also popular at that time. If I had any pen-pals, they apparently did not impress me because I don't remember any.

We grew up during a period when vaccines were being developed to combat many of the diseases that have since almost been eradicated. Back then the county nurse and other health officials were dispersed to schools to administer injections for polio, or we had to go to the county courthouse. I remember being lined up in the hallway by class to receive our shots. We also participated in helping to eradicate it by collecting donations for March of Dimes. We were each given a cardboard card with slots for actual dimes and were asked to collect enough dimes to fill each slot.

As a child of God, I always tried to maintain a humble spirit and was never a fighter. I endured a lot, but I do remember the one fight I got into during all my years of school – not proud of it, but it happened. I don't even remember why we fought but it was in the middle school years (6-8 grade) during the last period before school dismissal. I vividly remember, several people were cheering my opponent on to beat me up. Well, this smart girl found the long ponytail she had and worked my way to victory or until we were separated.

Chapter 8:

Courtship/ Company Keeping

(Dating for you young folk)

My folks didn't believe in that courting at a young age stuff. I remember the first boy I "liked" turned out to be my cousin so that was the end of that. The first person I called my real boyfriend was a guy from a rival school whom I met him at the local Christmas parade. That relationship never really got off the ground. However, not long after meeting him, I do remember their school came to our school to compete against our team in basketball. I bragged to my friends that I hoped my boyfriend would come. Sure enough, as we were sitting in our homeroom class, a group of guys from their school came down the hall, stopped in front of our opened classroom door, and looked in as if looking for someone. When I saw him, I was so shocked I felt like I could go through the floor. And then, when I heard him tell the guys with him, "there she is", I was speechless. When he spoke to me, I was so shocked that my teacher had to tell me to speak back. Oh well, so much for puppy love.

My first official boyfriend that I was allowed to have as "company" at our home was a local guy who was one grade ahead of me. I had gone to school with him all my life. One day he approached me during the lunch hour/recess and I think we walked around the high school building three or four times during that one hour just talking. I don't think we had sense enough to realize we could just stand and talk. He was allowed to visit me at my home, and we claimed a boyfriend-girlfriend relationship for a while – my first true love! By the time I started receiving company, we were in a new house with a separate living room, and I was officially "dating." This living room was strategically located next door to my parent's bedroom. Back in those days, when my daddy thought it was time for a guy to leave, he would knock on the wall. Old folks didn't believe in a guy staying at the house too late. If it got too quiet in the living room or if the guy didn't get the message to leave, daddy would walk past the door very fast in his underwear, push the door open, and keep walking. Guys usually got the hint then if they missed it the first time. I dated one other guy during those high school years, but it was nothing serious. My more serious relationship came later during my college years and thereafter.

I don't remember a lot about the dating habits of my siblings. I know one brother was smitten with a girl from a neighboring town/school. He really liked her and earned enough money to buy her a beautiful sweater for Christmas only to be dumped right after the holiday. One of my older sister's classmates came to visit her but I don't think that relationship ever got off the ground. My younger sister attracted the attention of a young man who wanted to be her special guy. When told they were cousins, he remarked, "Rooster, Rooster, Guinea, Guinea (that's a Guinea Hen you guys), cousin's love is good as any. Well--- it was not, and that was not to be. The boys always tried to keep their little business secret.

Chapter 9:
We Come This Far By Faith

Faith in God and striving to obey God in word and deed were always stressed in our family. My dad's father was a preacher and one of the founders of a Baptist Church in our community. From birth until we left home, our parents set guidelines for us from obeying the commandments, to living a Godly life, to attending church regularly, and actively participating in church activities. As far back as I can remember, we were a two-denomination family. My daddy and some members of our family were devout Baptists. My mama grew up in the Baptist Church but later united with the Church of God in Christ where she faithfully served until death. Several members of our family attended service with her under the COGIC umbrella.

Because our family was so large, it took two trips to get everybody to Sunday School and Church every Sunday. Since we went to two different churches with different starting and ending times, this worked out well. One group went, then the second group followed. All the girls originally went to church with my mama and the boys went with my daddy. Over the years, some changed denominations but still were required to maintain the regular church attendance and participation.

Few black churches had a baptismal pool in those days so those who accepted Christ and were candidates for baptism were taken to the river or creek for baptizing. As a child, I was baptized in Strong River and later in a baptismal pool at a local church during adulthood.

The Church of God in Christ (COGIC) was established in 1907 as a Holiness Pentecostal Christian denomination. Today, it is the largest Pentecostal denomination in the United States with churches in several foreign countries and widely accepted. That was not always the case. The denomination espoused to outpouring of the Holy Ghost as demonstrated by speaking in tongues unknown to oneself according to the will of God. As such, many of the established religions rejected this "new" teaching and members were ostracized, discriminated against, and outright laughed at and abused. Varying discernments among some of the early leaders, as well as Jim Crow laws that forbid black and whites from attending church together, led to the church being divided into Church of God in Christ (COGIC), Church of Christ Holiness (COCH), and Assemblies of God.

COGIC is where I received my spiritual foundation and where my membership remains today. As a small child, we studied the Bible in Sunday School, learned the Books of the Bible, did Bible drills, and were taught in the Sunshine Band and Young People Willing Workers (YPWW) departments. We participated in every program with speeches and songs. Our founding Pastor, Elder Samuel Quinn, even tried to teach a few of us how to play the piano; I don't think anybody caught on. We had lots of fun trying.

I took a hiatus from COGIC during my pre-teen/ early teen years and attended church with my daddy. At that time, COGIC was known for holding service for a long time (most of the day, and then night service). Because some of my friends, and siblings, who attended the Baptist church got home early, I didn't want to stay in church all day either. If the truth be known, they got home early enough to watch the then-popular show "Tarzan" on television --- and I wanted to see it too. Sad, I know, but it is the truth.

During my time at the Baptist Church, I actively participated in Sunday School and the church choir. My favorite Sunday School teacher there was Mr. Percy McIntosh. Of all the things he shared with us, the one thing I'll never forget is that he stressed to the members of our class that they should appreciate and be thankful for their parents, even if their dads were the town drunks. We routinely did Bible drills which helped me to learn more about the Bible. I was not there very long but I remember singing in the choir and going with the choir to sing at other churches. Although it was not a large choir, I remember once the entire choir traveling to a singing in a Volkswagen bug owned by one of the choir members. During that time, I learned more about God but never fully surrendered to enjoy that personal relationship with Him. Back at Grace Temple, I accepted Christ as my personal Savior and began working more earnestly in the Church.

Revivals at our church could last one to two weeks, all of which began on Sunday with "dinner on the ground." The ladies of the Church prepared "boxes" of homemade goodies (fried chicken, ham, beef, chicken and dumplings, dressing, potato salad, spaghetti, macaroni and cheese, all kinds of cakes and pies, and even goat) that were served out of the trunk of their cars or on tables that had been built under the shade trees since most black churches did not have a fellowship hall or kitchen at the time.

Over the years, we learned which cooks specialized in which dish and, even if we got a plate of food from one cook, sometimes we went to another to get that special piece of cake, pie, dressing, or chicken and dumplings. We almost always got a plate from my mama's box because she didn't want us "going around acting like we were hungry" but enjoyed goodies from the other ladies as well. We learned which cook to avoid if they did not have foods we liked. After church service, the dinner was served as we lined up and went from vehicle to vehicle or table to table. We then sat on benches that had been brought out of the church, on sheets/quilts placed on the ground under the shade tree, or on blankets on the back of the flatbed truck to enjoy our meal.

One year, during the opening of revival, as the ladies prepared plates to pass to the waiting recipients, one of the ladies we children didn't consider one of the better cooks, had prepared a plate and was ready to pass it to the next person waiting in line. As I stood in line at the next vehicle, one of my fellow church members pushed me toward her and told me there was a plate for me. That mother passed the plate to me and since I did not want to hurt her feelings, I took it. Now with that plate full of food, no one else was going to give a child another plate ----so I was stuck. To this day, I remember not enjoying my meal that I had waited for all year long.

Just like revival at any other church, we had people who came to the opening of our revival strictly for the plates of food they got. There were even people in the community that were notorious for getting two or more plates and carrying them to their car and then coming back to enjoy a plate while at the church. It was quite interesting to see these people leaving the church with the back dashboard of their cars lined with plates of food. Often people would get plates for family members who chose not to attend church but wanted to share in the revival meal. Our church was always known for serving good food – and it still is. We have had people comment that they come to Grace Temple "just to eat."

We had some dynamic speakers/evangelists sharing the Word during the revivals. Sometimes they were local people and sometimes they were from other cities or even other states. The most memorable revival for me was the year I accepted the Lord as my personal Savior and experienced the Baptism of the Holy Ghost. Even though I had been going to church all my life, had a Christian family, was taught to be a good person, and tried to live a godly life, I had not fully surrendered my will to God's will. For some reason I felt that going to and participating in church, reading my Bible, and treating people right made me right with the Lord. I felt this made me strong enough to resist the vices of Satan and defeat him. I was wrong!! I was naïve enough to think I could count the lies I told or sins I committed each day and make sure I did fewer the next day.

Yearning to know more about and to get closer to God, I didn't realize I had a pharisee-mentality – I felt I had to follow the Law to the letter to be saved. Only when I learned that no human achievement, no work of righteousness, or personal merit could save me did I come to acknowledge the Law as a keeper, and realized that only by confessing my sins and believing in Jesus Christ was I able to gain that personal relationship with God AND salvation through Jesus Christ. I have never chosen to go back. I'm not saying that I have been perfect or have not made mistakes since that day because I certainly have.

Because of my personal relationship with God, I realized that I can be forgiven and continue to grow in Christ. Without my faith in and dependence on God, I could not have made it over the years. So many challenges I encountered, some that really knocked me down to the ground, were not able to defeat me because I now have a Savior on my side, and He is stronger than I am, and He fights for me.

I have been blessed to serve the Lord in my local church as a member of the choir, church secretary, assistant secretary, member of the Finance Committee, Young People Willing Workers (YPWW) teacher, teacher for the junior Sunday School class and teacher of the Adult Sunday School class where I continue to teach. I have also served as Vice President and President of the Program Committee for my local church. At the district level, I was blessed to sing with the choir for a short time and to serve as District Secretary under the administration of two District Superintendents. I continue to support and work with the District churches when called upon.

Over the years, I have planned and executed trips for our congregation, both locally and out-of-state. On one of our trips via charter bus to Dallas Texas, the bus broke down in the middle of traffic. We were able to pull off to the side of the road where we had to wait hours for repairs. Unable to disembark the bus, I came up with some games/activities for the group to play and it made the time go by much faster. On another trip, we ventured to Peps Point in Hattiesburg, MS where the brothers of the Church barbequed while the children enjoyed the water slide, paddle boats, mini-golf, swimming, and other activities. We once joined with another local church for an adventure to one of our state parks where we had a great time. Those were the days.

Growing up in the COGIC, we were limited in the activities in which we could participate. Not only was wearing pants taboo, short-dresses were a no-no. I remember one incident when a young sister came to church wearing what was deemed too short by the church missionary. Mother proceeded to take this young lady outside and pulled the hem out of that dress to lengthen it – clothes had bigger hems in those days than they do now. Because of respect for the missionary and the desire to live a saved life, both parent and child submitted to this correction. Wouldn't advise anybody to try that these days. Over the years, some things have evolved. I do remember one year my local church played a game of baseball against the members of my family. There were many days of fun playing volleyball and enjoying food and activities for the children at church, especially following Vacation Bible School week.

Just like any other church, we have had our share of challenges over the years, as did I personally, but the Lord brought us through. When our founding pastor passed and the State Church assigned a new, younger pastor for our congregation, not everyone was enthusiastic about the change and there was some resistance. At one time during my younger years, we had a church bus and we traveled together to other churches and activities. I don't remember what happened to that bus, but we didn't have it very long.

Because of the beliefs of our COGIC denomination: speaking in tongues, guitar, drum, and tambourine playing, holy dancing, females not wearing pants, and not participating in a lot of extracurricular activities, we were often criticized. Don't even mention feet-washing or greeting the Saints with a holy kiss. You young people are not familiar with that. The Saints actually greeted each other with a holy kiss (that's not a sloppy, wet, tongue kiss, but a physical kiss with lips tucked in). Members of COGIC became the brunt of jokes by non-believers, and other denominations who did not understand our worship. Over the years, some of these things have been incorporated into the worship service of those same denominations as we have learned to praise God together.

Although I moved to a couple of nearby cities/towns during my adulthood, I never again moved my church membership but have faithfully continued to actively serve. During the latter years of my mother's life, when I came from the city to attend service, I would pick her up for church because her eyesight began to become not so clear, especially at night. We were often the first one to arrive at church and often the last to leave since I served on the finance committee. We had a lot of good conversations during those short trips which I appreciated then and made memories which I will forever cherish. Today, she remains the most influential person in my spiritual journey. Leading by example in word and deed, she was the wind beneath my wings – my SHEro!!!

Chapter 10:

Trip Down Memory Lane (Part 3)

CHILDHOOD STORIES

Childhood disputes occur in every family, and ours was no different. Once two of my brothers got into an argument and one threw a hatchet at the other and hit him in the back of the head --- splitting his head open. Not funny at the time, but we later would recall with humor that as we told him, he apparently thought he was Daniel Boone throwing his hatchet to split a tree as was the opening of the Daniel Boone show that was popular at that time.

Another adventure, purely accidental, happened when I cut my sister's ankle with a double-blade axe. On one of our many trips to find and cut down bundles of twigs for yard brooms or "brush-brooms" as we called them, which we used to sweep the yard. To accomplish this task, one person had to pull down and hold the tall twig/branch while a second person cut it at the base with an axe. While my sister was standing on the branch/twig to hold it in place, she slipped just as I brought the axe down to cut it. Needless to say, that axe cut into her ankle and then she had to limp, with our help, from the woods to the house cut and bleeding. Thankfully, I was not good with the axe and no permanent damage was done. I'm sorry Mary!!

Another childhood memory was being pulled out of a moving truck. During one of our rides in the pulp wood truck, while daddy was driving, we came to a major curve on our road, still referred to as "the curve". I don't remember where we were going or why, but I vividly remember the door of the passenger side of the truck flew open. My oldest sister Stella was sitting by the door with me in the middle seat. As she was being thrown out of the vehicle, she reached for something to hold onto. She grabbed me and out we both went, landing on the gravel road. Thankfully, we did not make contact with the back tires of the truck and were not ran-over and we did not sustain any serious or permanent injuries.

Still another memory that was a bit traumatic for me. This happened when I was a small child, but I remember it quite well. My parents and the older children had gone to the field, and I was left to watch the younger children. Well, somebody had the idea that they would climb up the Chifforobe, a chest-like piece of furniture that had drawers on one side and a long space for hanging clothes on the other side. It was not full of clothes and when one of the children tried to climb up those drawers, the whole thing came tumbling down on top of us. We were not strong enough to lift it upright. Luckily, either my parents or one of the older siblings came from the field to get water and found us and rescued us from that unknown fate. No one was seriously injured thank the Lord, but we all got in trouble and had to pay for our mistake.

Another of my babysitting adventures: Left with those hard-headed children again, they would not listen to me. For some reason, they got into Madear's flour. I don't know if the plan was to cook later or just toss it around. Well, it so happened that the local nurse, a relative of ours (yes, I said a relative of ours -- figure that out), stopped by and we were all covered in flour. Mrs. Lee told them she was going to make some biscuits for us. Apparently one of our parents saw her drive up and came to see what she wanted and discovered our mess. I don't remember if we got a whipping or not, but I feel sure we did because we had wasted the groceries and made a big mess.

I shared the story earlier of how my sister Eva, inexperienced in using a new washing machine, got her hand/arm stuck in the wringer while trying to feed clothes through it and it rolled all the way up to her shoulder and our cousin Chuck (Charlie Babe) came by at that time, hit the release button, and saved her life as he proclaims to this day. Eva has always been pretty vocal (most folks thought she was quiet). Even when saying the Lord's prayer as a child, when she got to the part, "Deliver us from evil", she would say "Deliver us from Stella" as she thought they were saying her name – Eva.

As a small child, I always liked to follow the older children. On one such occasion, while getting water in a 55-gallon drum which was on a slide being pulled by a mule, there was an accident. The older children, as older kids will do, tried to make the mule go fast and jump a ditch. Standing at the front of the slide when the mule jumped the ditch, I tumbled over the top of that slide and luckily landed in the ditch while the slide, drum of remaining water, and all the kids on board, ran over me.

Again, God spared my life. Scars still cover my arm and leg today, but I had no serious injuries and no permanent damage.

My uncle had an old Model T car that was no longer running, and it became a play car for us, and we took turns pretending to drive. This old car had been pulled into the pasture and was missing a lot of parts. As I look back, I realize that it never dawned on us that there could be snakes and/or wasp nests or other creatures throughout the car ready to attack and harm us.   By God's grace and because of a praying mother, we never encountered a problem.

Growing up in a large family and lots of cousins and neighborhood kids, we always had somebody to play games with. In the early years, I remember going to my grandmother's brother's house where Madear and my great aunt would make t-cakes and visit while we played. Badminton, baseball, basketball, marbles, jump rope, jump board, checkers (Chinese and regular), etc. were all part of our growing experience. When we were young, the Sunday afternoon baseball game with the neighbors was on. As we got older and could afford more, board games and cards became a part of our entertainment as well. As we aged more and the grandchildren got big enough, our Sunday afternoon activity became volleyball. Because we always had lots of children flocking to our house, we were never short of people for the teams and a good game and lot of fun could be guaranteed.

Not knowing that I did not have perfect vision, I went through eleven years of school without glasses. I don't know who decided that my eyesight was not what it should be, but apparently it was determined to be lacking. During the summer before my senior year of high school, I got my first pair of glasses. Since we did not have a lot of money, my first pair of glasses was purchased by the Lions Club. Putting them on for the first time, I remember how amazed I was at how much better everything looked and the improvement in my eyesight. I remember walking around just looking at the sky and all kind of things through my new glasses and comparing the view without them. You don't know what you don't know, and you can't see what you can't see. Chew on that!

Even though I was a young child, when my great-grandfather, Poppa Manuel (Emanuel Carter) died, I remember the day of his funeral. I remember it not because I knew him that well but because what happened that day was very traumatic for me. On that day, my Aunt Rosemary and her husband Ray left to return home to Chicago and took my younger sister Mary with them but did not take me. As a young child, I did not understand why they did not want to take me but took my sister. I remember crying, kicking, and screaming on the back of somebody's pickup truck we were riding on when they left immediately after the funeral. I did not understand she was not leaving for good; I just remember feeling rejected and not wanting my sister to leave me.

I went to the State Fair once or twice in all my childhood years. I remember riding on the back of Uncle Barney's pickup truck. We didn't indulge in any of the rides or other activities because we only had enough money for admission. We walked around looking at everything, got the free biscuit and syrup at the syrup-making booth, and whatever other freebies (usually a plastic rain cap/bonnet) that they gave away.

My only trip to the movies as a young child was to the movie theater in Mendenhall. During those years, the races did not sit together. The Black section of the theater was upstairs, and the White section was downstairs. I don't remember what movie we saw or who I went with; we were just thrilled at the experience. So thrilled that it didn't resonate with me that we were being discriminated against.

Some teenagers were allowed to have parties/dances at their homes, but we generally weren't allowed to go. I remember once I went to a party with my sisters and brothers. The menu generally consisted to cheese and crackers and punch and maybe some type of sandwich halves. The music was from records played on a record player or from the radio. I remember having my first dance with a boy that night. He was not my boyfriend, but he was a pretty good dancer.

Back in those days, record players and those "vinyl records" or the radio provided musical entertainment. Although I do not remember my siblings doing it, many of our friends and neighbors would call the local radio station and request specific songs be played. I do remember an incident where one person called the station and requested the disc jockey play "Boston can feel more", not realizing the name of the song was "Ball of Confusion."

There actually were more merchant stores in our small town when I was growing up than there are now. In addition to the stores in the town area and one located near our school there was also a rolling grocery store. A guy they called Croffit came by once a week with his UPS styled truck. He sold everything from groceries to penny candy which we sometimes bought, to sodas, and some of everything. There was also a salesman that came by monthly I believe selling Watkins brand flavor/products.

OUTHOUSE STORIES

Stories of the outhouse days are too numerous to list but I'll share a few of them. Not only did we have outhouses at home, but the Black schools also had no indoor toilets during my first few years of school. Before our new school was built, we used the bathroom outdoors. I remember once my oldest sister, Stella, apparently not wanting to sit but choosing to stand on the seat in the outhouse, dropped one of her shoes through the opening of the toilet seat. No one bothered to search for that shoe; it became a casualty of the outhouse.

Since there were few people with indoor plumbing during my growing up years, there was no shame in the game. My first memory of the outhouse was of a tin building with one-seat. If there was an emergency to go and that outhouse was occupied, you had to hit the woods. This occurred more times than you would think. As our family grew, so did the outhouse. We became a two-seater family. Toilet paper varied, everything from the Sears catalog to the weekly Grits Paper (newspaper), etc.

Probably one of the most memorable outhouse stories was carried out by our brother L. J. He was always a strong-willed child, a bit stubborn, not very patient, and could get a heated temper in a hurry. Did I mention the outhouse was one of the few places you could have some privacy and lock the door. Well, one day nature called, and L. J. headed to the outhouse to answer the call. Unfortunately, my brother Robert Earl was already there. After waiting quite a while, L. J. decided he would

84

help Robert Earl speed up by setting small brush fires surrounding the outhouse and "smoking him out". It worked, but he got into trouble for starting fires and almost hurting his brother.

When we finally got indoor plumbing, we had only one bathroom for our large family so, as you could imagine, if you got in an emergency situation and someone was already in the bathroom, you still had to hit the outhouse or the woods. We felt like we had come up in the world being able to use the toilet without going outside and taking a bath in a real bathtub rather than a number three tub.

VACATION FOR REAL?

Family vacations for us meant days when we didn't have to go to the field. We loudly complained to daddy if we had to work on Labor Day which of course was during the harvest season. Since we didn't have a vehicle large enough to haul our group, travel was limited, to say the least. My mama always wanted more for her children so as we grew older, she determined that we would see something other than the small town we called home.

After the older kids left home, Madear decided that Father's Day weekend would be a good time for us to get away as a group. That weekend became a standing appointment for our annual family trip. One of our first trips was to the Mississippi Gulf Coast (Gulfport/ Biloxi beach area). This was an interesting choice of vacation spots since prior to the late 60s, the beaches were not open to Black people. Even with the Biloxi Wade-in civil rights protests in 1963 and the passage of the Civil Rights Act of 1964, Biloxi beaches were segregated until 1968. With the front of their pickup truck full and the rest on the back of the truck and the older kids in their vehicles with their families, my folks hit the road. That first trip and some thereafter were day trips only. Daddy later brought a large blue and white passenger van, and everybody was now able to ride inside, and we kept rolling. I remember one year Uncle Barney and his wife went on the trip with us. I still have pictures of him knee deep in the water with the legs of his coveralls rolled up, baring those legs. They had a ball as they had never done much traveling either. Playing in the Gulf and on the sandy beaches opened a new world to us that we had never experienced. Over the years, we had many, many families and friends join us for the annual trip while it was a day trip and even when we extended it to overnight. Not until several years later did we actually book hotel rooms and stay overnight. Talk about "hog heaven." We were living then, and everybody was thrilled to not only be able to enjoy the beach but also the comfort of a hotel room and the luxury of a swimming pool, even though most of us could not swim at the time.

Over the years, we ventured to other parts of the state. We discovered the Pep's Point Water Park in Hattiesburg, Mississippi, and traveled there a few times. The kids were now enjoying places and things that we never imagined. The park had a lot to offer: we had our own pavilion with a barbeque grill, paddle boats, swimming, water slides, mini-golf, basketball, volleyball, etc. Another year we traveled to the Military Park in Vicksburg, Mississippi. We toured the park by car and later visited several of the monuments and artifacts. The park was large and very interesting. We were not informed in advance of a tradition at the Park of firing the cannons at noon. When this happened, several members of our party were visibly shaken and were looking for a place to hide when the cannons were fired.

As families grew and kids got older, this country family spread its wings and ventured further to adjoining states for our family trips. This opened a whole new world for many of us – some who had never been out of state before. One of our first out-of-state trips was to Memphis, Tennessee. Our hotel had an inside pool which came in handy as it was storming the afternoon after we visited several landmarks the first morning of our trip. Although I don't remember a lot about this trip, one memorable thing still remains with me today. As we were headed to our hotel, suddenly two cars engaged in road rage came barreling past our line of cars. The occupants of those vehicles were yelling and cursing at each other, and we expected to hear and see gunfire at any moment. We quickly slowed down so we would not get in the line of fire in case gunfire broke out and to make sure they were out of sight before we proceeded to our destination.

Another out-of-state trip was to New Orleans, Louisiana. Normally, we travel together on these family trips – a caravan of cars. This particular year, a couple of novice drivers struck out on their own only to turn in the wrong direction when they got to the Interstate. They headed north for several miles before realizing they should be going south to reach New Orleans. They still get teased today about getting lost. Our reserved hotel yielded a facility undergoing renovations, no place to park (would have had to find parking on the street) and a pool that was not open. After a bit of discussion, we were upgraded to another one of their properties which met the specifications of our reservation and had much better amenities and an indoor pool. Since valet parking was not a part of our reservation and none of the drivers were prepared to pay it, I had the good pleasure of charging the valet fees for all our vehicles for our entire stay to my credit card. Did I mention our caravan generally consists of 8-10 vehicles, and sometime more? In the spirit of good customer relations and a nice demand letter from me, those charges were reimbursed.

Okay, this next story happened after we grew up – full adults, with children of our own. One year, the girls in the family (and a couple of grand girls) planned and executed a shopping trip to Alabama. It was a GREAT trip. We had a couple of rooms for our stay and the ride to and from Alabama was "a hoot." We bought lots of stuff and then took everything to our rooms to display and model for the group. We had so much stuff that the baggage carrier atop the van/SUV was full. But a never-to-be -forgotten incident happened on the return trip home at night. A very lively discussion ensued about a lady we all knew who was very vibrant, outspoken, and just fun to be around. We talked and laughed and talked and laughed some more. We weren't paying attention to the road and going with the flow of traffic (I was not driving) and little did we know we had incorrectly taken an exit when we should not have. Honestly, we were surrounded by semi-trucks and did not see the directional signs. After riding and laughing for many miles, we realized this dark road we were on was not where we should be.   When we finally saw some road signs, we realized we had been traveling south when we should have been going west and were close to Hattiesburg (about 80 miles in the wrong direction) when we should have been headed toward Jackson. At this point, we had no choice but to continue to Hattiesburg and take the state highway 49 from Hattiesburg back to Jackson/ Pinola. We determined that we would not share outside the group what had happened. What happens in Vegas stays in Vegas. Well, it has already been shared so I'm not spilling any new tea.

HOLIDAYS

Holidays were and still are special around our house. Again, I don't think we realized, or it didn't bother us, that we were poor. For Easter, we always attended early morning Sunrise Service celebrating the resurrection of our Savior, Jesus Christ. An Easter program was always a part of that service. Of course, we were required to participate on the program, either by saying a poem, participating in a skit/play, or singing. Even the smallest ones had to say something, if nothing more than: "What are you looking at me for, I didn't come to stay; I just came to let you know today is Easter Day." We always dyed hard-boiled eggs, hid, and hunted them after church. This tradition was a huge deal with the children and continues to be carried on today, except we now use plastic, colored eggs filled with candy and even money. Since we lived in the country, we always had a wide space to hide the eggs so, depending on who hid them, the hunt could take a minute. Following the egg hunt, it was time to pull out the salt and pepper and devour those eggs. We could always tell who ate the most eggs because the smell from passing gas soon permeated the air. We always felt sorry for the teachers the Monday following Easter Sunday because they had a room-full of children who had indulged in real, hard-boiled eggs the day before.

At Thanksgiving a festive time was had by all. It marked the near end of the harvest season, meaning we were almost through working in the field and the holiday season (Thanksgiving, Christmas, winter) was on the horizon. We had a break in school and there was always so much good food to enjoy. We really loved Thanksgiving. A tradition was later set that we rotated Thanksgiving dinner, going from the family-home house to the home of one of the siblings and then to the next. We continue that tradition to this day.

Growing up, Christmas at our house was different from many, but some activities similar to those of many of our neighbors. Our tree was not store-bought. We went into the woods each year to find a tree we liked. Just as we didn't have money to buy a tree, we didn't have money to buy decoration; therefore, our decoration was homemade. I remember picking those red berries and holly leaves to string together to go on the tree. We sometime made paper decorations and hung them by thread. There were no gifts placed under the tree. When we did get gifts for Christmas, they were hidden (we figured out they were hidden in the loft) until Christmas morning. We tried staying up Christmas Eve as long as we could, but somehow, we never stayed up long enough or got up early enough to catch our parents putting the presents out. We had fun singing Christmas songs, reading books, and eating snacks the night before Christmas.

Everybody always got an individual bag with an apple, an orange, some candy, and nuts. As we got older, daddy gave the older children $1.00 and took us to town where we could spend that dollar on our Christmas gift—and we did. Prior to that, gifts range from cap guns, Yo-yos, marbles, cowboy hats, spinning tops, and bald-headed, white dolls. If Black dolls were available at that time, they were few and far between and we didn't see any. My sister Eva reminded me of a unique, memorable Christmas gift she and my sister Stella received one year. Our uncle came to them and told them, "Girls, I have a Christmas present for you." That Christmas present turned out to be a pair of boy's high-top shoes for each of them --- and they had to wear them! I shall never forget the infamous gift my daddy bought one year. He thought he was doing a good deed and purchasing perfume for all the girls in the family. That perfume proved to be a spray can of FDS (feminine deodorant spray). He was not allowed to pick our gifts on his own again, but we all had fresh bottoms.

Christmas food was the best. Madear started cooking about a week before Christmas. She had a signature jam cake that she made every year --- and everybody loved it. She also made a layer cake with cooked, chocolate frosting. Again, everybody wanted a piece. Along with the traditional Christmas meal, we had lots of cakes and other sweets for a few days. During this time of year, relatives would come by and help us enjoy those desserts as well. We often visited other family members and shared in their goodies as well.

Weekends around our place, after all the work was done, were always fun. Eating, playing games, and just laughing with a big family was wonderful. Generally, Saturday nights were our treat time. We would make a no-bake chocolate, oatmeal cookie almost weekly. We also made peanut brittle and taffy. When daddy got hooked on tuna fish, it was on. We added those sandwiches to our Saturday night menu. Tuna sandwiches were a delicacy. This was our party time. We didn't have birthday celebrations and there were no gifts or parties, so this was our time.

When we got older, we began to celebrate other holidays like the Fourth of July and New Years with firecrackers, sparklers, and the like.

Chapter 11:

Gone But Not Forgotten

MADEAR

MADEAR, that word says it all – my dear mama!! I have never known or even met a person with a more humble, loving, devoted spirit who unconditionally loved and easily forgave everybody. From my earliest years, I remember her sharing, serving, and giving of herself to anybody who needed her – from her parents, to her siblings, to her husband and children, grandchildren, neighbors, church family, relatives, and friends—and there were a lot of us to share with. I couldn't understand how the woman managed. From Madear at home, Miss Anna Lee in the neighborhood and community, to Mother Banks at church, she had the admiration and respect of all who knew her. Neighborhood children flocked to our home because they knew she loved kids and welcomed them all. When I look back over the years, it had to be only by the grace of God that she was able to do the many things she did and still maintain her sanity.

As the mother of 13 children and devoted wife of a farmer, she could have settled for being a tired and depressed housewife because she had a lot going on.

However, she was the exact opposite – always leading, always the disciplinarian, always sharing in activities of family, church, and friends. I don't ever remember her displaying a sad countenance or crying in front of us because of her circumstances or the way she had been treated or mistreated. Mind you, she could raise her voice and leave no doubt as to what her intention was, but it was never in a spiteful or inhumane manner even though the odds were stacked against her as a poor, black woman with a large family in rural Mississippi. This sweet lady could be a stern disciplinarian, having to discipline some more than others.

Madear was usually the first to hit the floor in the morning. Sometimes she was the last to go to bed at night, although that was not her normal bedtime. A lot of people went to bed "with the chicken", which meant they turned in early. During my growing-up years, we always had a hot breakfast.   The smell of homemade biscuits, farm-raised bacon or sausage, eggs from our laying hens, homemade molasses (syrup), rice, grits, and gravy permeated every room of the house causing us to eagerly get out of bed. Her discernment of how much to prepare to feed this crew was a mystery to me, but she had it down pat and knew exactly how many biscuits to cook. We may not have always had what we wanted to eat, but we never missed a meal. A hot breakfast before school and a hot meal waiting for us when we returned was the norm at our house. We raised or grew the bulk of the food we consumed (sausage/bacon from the hogs, milk from the cows, eggs from the chicken, and fresh or canned fruits and vegetables). As children, we were never asked what we wanted to eat as is the case with children today. We ate whatever my mama cooked and enjoyed it or waited until the next meal if she was serving something we didn't like, AND we didn't dare go back into the kitchen and try to fix something else that we liked.

Life in the South was hard, so Madear learned to utilize any and everything available to help make ends meet. She painstakingly made lye soap, made quilts for our beds, cooked syrups from sugar cane, went to the fields and completed all the fieldwork everybody else did, canned fruits and vegetables for the family to eat over the winter months, and never did she complain. With the number of girls she had, as we started to reach puberty, personal items were scarce. Some of the personal items were homemade until we were able to purchase them from the store. Hey, we did what we had to do to maintain our cleanliness. We were taught to be good girls, to be confident in who we were, to be proud of our body and our looks, and to love and care for other girls/women— lifting them up. The unconditional love and friendship among black women were very obvious. They looked out for each other and their children, and they taught us girls to have that same caring spirit.

Many people in the neighborhood looked to her for medical advice. Even though she had no formal training, giving birth to and rearing all those children over the years prepared her to deal with almost every illness and the prevention of illness where possible. You could say she was the neighborhood doctor. There were midwives who delivered babies at home at that time, but I don't ever remember her delivering a baby. I do remember my uncle telling someone to do whatever my mama said to do because he trusted her as much as he did any doctors.One incident I recall was when a neighbor's son was having major stomach problems and they had done all they could do to no avail. They then called for my mama to come and check on him. Hearing his symptoms, she grabbed her hot water bottle and headed to their house and gave that young man an enema. He was up an about in no time at all and he had no further complaints. We were blessed to have access to this great home-healthcare not just because there so many of us but also because professional medical treatment for Black people was minimal or substandard, if it existed at all. The one time I went to the doctor growing up was with two or three siblings who were all sick. Apparently, the home remedies hadn't kicked that bug, so we went to the doctor. I remember the Caucasian doctor looking at (not really examining) one child and declaring he had the flu and then, shocking to me, declaring that "all the others had the same thing" without even taking one temperature. We all got the same medicine, and only by God's grace, did we survive.

Even with all those tasks at hand, Madear was a strong disciplinarian – not sparing the rod when it was needed when someone was disobedient when told to do something or God forbid, they did something they had been told not to do or something they knew was wrong. She never chased anybody to discipline them. She knew most of us were afraid of the dark and would come into the house and go to bed sooner or later. Somehow, she knew when the guilty party went to bed and felt comfortable going to sleep. Just when they thought it safe, they felt the bed covers being snatched away and felt the sting of those green switches that we ourselves had to cut and gather. Innocent bedmates had to move quickly to avoid the punishment of the guilty offender. I've seen a guilty child try to go under the bed and that switch followed them.

Proven to be an outstanding homemaker, she was equally devoted to helping her children build a good educational foundation to prepare them for life and teaching them the Word of God so they could enjoy a personal relationship with God and prepare them for eternity. She was the epitome of a what a Christian should be. She never just sent us to Sunday School or Church – she took us!!! In addition to studying the written Word at home and attending church services, we were favored with gospel songs/music and preachers on radio and later television. Her labor was not in vain. God blessed her children to attain local, state, and national recognitions. Even more importantly, He called some to preach, teach, and evangelize the Gospel message and all to witness His Good News. Some were blessed to render service in the medical field as doctors, nurses and social workers, a lawyer in the legal field, teachers, truck drivers, factory supervisors, office workers etc.

As a child, she had to quit school, but many people attest to the fact that she was always a very smart person. After most of her children were grown and had left home, she went back to school and earned her GED (General Education Development) Certificate through the local community college. As the children left home and the manual labor dwindled, the farming subsided and Madear took a job as a cook with the local Head Start (known as Sophia Sutton then, Five County now). After attaining her Certificate, she became a Head Start teacher.

As I said earlier, a humbler person you would not meet. She was always putting others before herself. Even when she cooked, she made sure everybody else had a plate before she ate. I remember wondering to myself as I saw others do what I thought was taking advantage or her kindness why wouldn't she speak up and/or tell them where to go. She was confident in who she was as well as Whose she was, so it didn't matter what others said or thought. She often quoted the saying to us: "Just because someone calls you a dog does not mean you have to bark." She was filled with wisdom and shared many sayings/cliches which were inspired by or taken directly from the Scriptures. A couple others were: "When you meet up with a fool, let him go" and "if you can't say nothing good about somebody, don't say nothing at all."

Madear was a praying woman. She kept her husband and children before the Lord. I believe to this day that her prayers over us were what kept us healthy, safe, and protected. She trusted God and pleaded for us even when we became adults with families of our own. A very wise woman, she was not only a chaste keeper at home, but she also served as the clerk or secretary for our church for many years as well as the adult Sunday School Teacher.

Bad weather was the only thing I remember that bothered her. When there was a storm, she would tell us to sit still while the Lord was doing his work. If the weather got really bad during the night, she would wake us up and we had to get fully dressed till the storm passed. She trusted God but she didn't play about them storms.

Born in Simpson County where her parents and grandparents lived, Madear moved to the Mississippi Delta when her mother married a man from that area. She and her three sisters moved back to Simpson County when her mother and stepfather divorced. Her mother then married an older man who she later divorced (after Madear got married and had left home) before leaving the state and moving to Chicago, Illinois. Madear had the opportunity to follow other members of her family moving north to Chicago but chose to remain in

Mississippi because she didn't want to rear her children in the city.

A whole book could be dedicated to the life and times of this strong Black woman. No doubt she would have brought much more life and light to this world had her life not been snatched away in such a tragic manner. An automobile accident resulting from the foolishness of teenagers who chose to race their cars on a major highway with no regard for their life or the lives of others took her away from her beloved family and friends.

DADDY

Born and raised in central Mississippi, he was the 9th of 13 children. He was the baby of his biological mother who died when he was only nine months old. His dad remarried and he grew up with a stepmother who did not always favor the stepchildren. His dad, Paw-Paw Steve, was a farmer, a preacher, and operated a small store for a time. He was one of the founders of the New Zion Missionary Baptist Church where he is buried and where several family members still worship. The son of a Caucasian father who determined that he would be educated, PawPaw learned to read and write. He had several relatives who supported him but of course, in Mississippi, there were many haters because of his mixed-race. He raised my daddy and his siblings with a stern hand and in the fear of the Lord.

Daddy and Madear married when they were young. He joined the army and served two tours of duty for his county. A veteran of World War II, he attained the rank of Corporal Tech-5 (Sargent) before receiving an honorable discharge. During one of his overseas tours, he worked in the transportation area serving as a truck driver picking up and transporting the bodies, and oftentimes body parts of those killed in action. Not until years later did I understand his desire for alcohol as a way to deal with these unspeakable, deeply hidden memories. He was a proud veteran, serving on army bases in Mississippi, Georgia, New Jersey and California and tours oversea to Okinawa and the Philippines. On his tour to the Philippines, he survived one of the strongest land-falling storms recorded in history. This typhoon had sustained winds of 95-200 mph with gusts up to 255 mph. For his years of service, he was awarded the Asiatic Pacific Campaign Medal, World War II Victory Medal, Army of Operations Medal, and Philippine Independence Medal. This country boy proudly wore his WWII Veteran hat until he left this earth.

For most my life, Daddy worked as a farmer. Over the years, he also hauled pulp wood, worked at a meat packing plant, and worked on the construction of the International Airport in Jackson, MS. Along with my mama, he was always working to support his children and instilling in us strong work ethics and moral values. We often told him he worked us like slaves as the farm work was very hard and tiring. He and the boys cut and hauled pulp wood but we all, girls and boys, cut, hauled, split, and stacked wood for use in the fireplace and heaters. During harvest season, he would show up at the school around noon to collect his children for dismissal so we could work in the field during the afternoon. In the height of the season, we missed school to get the crops in. We endured full days working under the sun, only taking a break under the nearest shade tree to eat lunch which was a sandwich, some punch, and water. Cotton and cucumber crops were the most strenuous.

Often, we were "hired out" to work for other farmers. Once we worked for a fellow who had the timber cut on his land to get it prepared for farming. After the cutting and removing the biggest pieces of wood, we were hired to pick up the remaining limbs and stumps for a whopping $3 per day. We worked on the farms of uncles, cousins, neighbors, and even white people we didn't know. I remember occasionally after we finished picking cucumbers, daddy allowed us to sit atop the sacks on the back of the truck as we took them to the "vat" for sale. Once they were sold, we were sometime rewarded with a nickel which we immediately spent at one of the few local stores to purchase candy or snacks. He allowed us to do this and protected us even though he knew we were being discriminated against and that the merchants were watching our every move from the time we entered the store until the minute we left.

He made sure we got to church on Sundays even though we had to make two trips because we couldn't all fit in one car. He was a strong disciplinarian, but I think Madear had the major role there. I can't remember him ever whipping me – I guess I was just a good child; however, I remember one of my sisters getting a paddling with the checkerboard. I remember he and Madear limited the work we could do on Sunday. We had to get our ironing done on Saturday. My sister Eva used the Scripture found in Ephesians 6:4 (Fathers, provoke not your children to wrath) when daddy did something she did not like or thought he shouldn't have said or done. She would say, "Don't have me start wrath-ing." Apparently, they did a pretty good job of rearing us because they never had to keep running to the schoolhouse or jailhouse to rescue their children – not perfect by any means but parent-fearing and God-fearing!

Daddy taught us to fish and those who wanted to learn how to hunt. Hunting was something I never wanted to do. He bought hooks, lines, and sinkers and we attached them to the bamboo fishing pole we cut, and it was time to fish. Daddy was the only one who had a reel and rod for many years. We didn't buy much bait, but dug up earthworms or used discarded, unusable pieces of meat. I loved to fish, and I would bait my own hook but I never, till this day, got up the nerve to take the fish off the hook. Cleaning them bad boys was no fun but eating them was great.

He loved to hunt and eat rabbits, squirrels, racoon, possum, and deer—all that wild stuff. I hated cleaning (skinning) them. Never seemed like enough meat on the small game to make a meal but Madear could make a gravy with each that proved to be quite yummy – still not much meat so you know who got to eat that, which was fine by me. The boys in the family developed the love for hunting as well but not to the degree my daddy did. He took the girls hunting once and I think that was enough for him. He soon brought us out of the woods back to the road and told us to go home; I know it was enough for me. He was still trying to hunt at the age of 94. After we got on him about going off into the woods alone at that age and with his health issues, he then not-so-legally hunted from his truck parked on the side of the road.

Daddy always wanted somebody to comb or brush his hair, which he kept cut very low. He had a full head of hair until his death at almost 95 years old and didn't grey until late in life. He also had his own teeth until his demise. He loved coffee and would sometimes pour some from his cup into the saucer and let us kids take a sip. For you young'un, back then people poured coffee into saucers from their cups and drank from the saucers.

I'm not sure many people even use saucers today. When he didn't want to share, he fed into the stereotype saying that drinking coffee would make you black. Society, and the South especially, did not make us feel proud to be Black so that was not a flattering statement.

In his down time, Daddy loved to play the harmonica when we were growing up. He could really play it but for some reason did not play in his later years. Another hobby he enjoyed was that of playing the card games solitary, gin rummy, and canasta and playing dominos. Solitary was the only game I mastered. He taught some of my siblings the card games but mostly the grandchildren how to play dominos. They are still playing today.

Even though he was the father of many, he liked to try to "hang out with the boys." Once after an outing with the boys, he came home a bit tipsy. When Madear got on him, he left the house in a hurry and proceeded to drive off --- drove straight into the woods. Thankfully, he was not injured; can't say the same about the car.

MAW MAW MISSOURI

A lot of my memories of my grandmother are from her annual visits and the letters/communications she regularly sent, often with a box of clothes for us. By the time I came along, she was living in Chicago, and we so looked forward to her visits. She had a disposition similar to that of my mother: a loving person but a strict disciplinarian. She didn't play either!

The one thing we kids found humor in was that she was a snorer. She could literally be asleep on one end of the house, and we would hear her snoring on the other end. I don't think I've ever encountered but one other person in my lifetime that could snore like Maw-Maw. I think she came to visit us every summer and for many years she rode the train unless she caught a ride with a relative traveling down here. As she got older, she took to the airways and flew to see us. Married twice, she produced four daughters and one son who died very young. She later left the South, moving to Chicago, Illinois, where she lived with my aunt and her husband. She remained with them until she died.

AUNT MARY (CAN)

Daddy had a sister named Mary that we called "Aunt Can" who could not hear or speak audibly. Back in those days they were referred to as deaf and dumb, a term that was discarded because of the stigma attached to it. I'm not sure how she became deaf, but I do know that she was in a fire and suffered severe burns. She was a fantastic cook – people longed to taste one of her cakes. She was a big hit at Revival time – always had to have a plate from her. She was also an entrepreneur: all the children called her the "Candy Lady." She sold candy from her home, in the neighborhood, and at church. One of my favorites was a coconut bar that had three different color stripes, pink, white and blue or green.

Although she could not speak or hear, she knew everybody's business. She was very observant (very nosy), and she would converse by writing. For a time, she attended the Mississippi School for the Deaf where she learned to use sign language; unfortunately, nobody else in the family knew how to sign. She was married to a guy who always brought humor to our lives. His name was R. D. but everybody called him "De'Bo." He really was a hoot, telling stories (fables) about his days as a cowboy and all kinds of wild western stories. He was a slick dresser and thought he was a ladies' man, but he always took good care of my Aunt Can. I couldn't understand a lot of things she said to him but when she got upset with him, you knew. She plainly called him "fool" on more than one occasion.

They had no children, so we were like her children. She made dresses for the girls that we did not like because they looked so old-fashioned, but we had to wear them. Some of us would occasionally stay at their house overnight. Their beds were so high that we literally had to climb up into them. I was sometimes afraid if I stayed by myself because I slept alone in a big bed in the front room leading to the front door of the house. As a child, I was also fearful that their whole house was going to sink into the ground. Their water well was a couple of feet from the back door. If you looked into the well, you could see the water (about 10-15 feet from the top of the well). Aunt Can was a stickler for cleanliness, and she kept her house immaculate. She always went to church with a starched, well-pressed dress or suit and always wore her hat and makeup. Since she only lived a few houses away from us, she visited us often and we visited her often.

ROBERT EARL

Robert Earl was my second oldest brother. He was a special child from birth, the result of Madear being shot while she was carrying him. As my cousin Willie (who we called Jr.) shared the story, he, daddy and a pregnant Madear were traveling to the store when they passed a neighbor's house where the father and his son were having a dispute in the front yard. Just as they passed the house, one of the two fired a shot from a rifle which hit the car my family was traveling in. Not realizing the bullet hit the car, they continued the drive. Willie said

Madear did not say anything until they had gotten off that road and traveled a distance up the highway and then shared that she had been shot. Robert Earl was born with some physical and mental impairments. He completed elementary school and began high school before he quit school. He had difficulty keeping up in class and could have benefited from individualized instruction or special education but that was not offered in schools back then. Willie maintained an ought against that father and son even into his old age, declaring that if they were still alive, he wanted to kill them himself.

When Madear went back to school to get her GED, Robert Earl went also. Together, they attended night classes offered at the local junior college. When the course ended, she took the test and earned her certificate, but he did not, and he didn't want to continue studying by himself.

He was always expected to work like the rest of us, sometime a little slower but he did his share. He worked on the farm, plowing behind the mule and then driving the tractor when we finally were able to afford one. He helped haul pulp wood, and anything else the rest of the crew did. During one period of time, he went through the neighborhood selling a newspaper that was really popular in the rural area called Grits. The company provided a sack-type backpack that hung around his neck in which he carried the papers. We enjoyed getting and reading the newspaper (and the extra toilet paper for the outhouse). I have no idea how much he was paid; but he was paid.

He and his pawpaw (Steve Banks, Sr.) were big television-watching buddies, so they spent a lot of time together. Later, he also enjoyed doing word-find puzzles and listening to his radio in his spare time. We teased him because he would always wear socks and shoes every day, never going barefoot even though we were in the heart of the country where everybody went bare foot at some time.

Even though he had labored breathing much of the time, he would sneak around to make and smoke a cigarette made of "rabbit tobacco." He got in trouble many a day for trying to smoke. When he became an adult and had money of his own, he would buy cigarettes and try to hide them from my mama and smoke when nobody saw him. He never married or had children of his own but loved children and played with and favored everybody's children, treating my youngest sister's children just like they were his.

He survived the vehicle accident in which Madear was killed. Tragically, he died of smoke inhalation when the family-home house burned some years later.

Chapter 12:

To Be Continued...

I mentioned in the introduction that the main reason for writing this book is to pass on knowledge/experiences that will otherwise be lost. Our family has always gathered somewhere in one form or another on Sundays to fellowship and share. While adults and children frequently share conversations today, that was not the case when I was growing up. When adults sat around and talked, children were not only not allowed to be in the same room, but they weren't even allowed to be inside the house. We didn't have electronic games and other toys to entertain us, but we found lots of things to do to have fun, while staying "in a child's place." If an adult thought you were trying to listen to their conversation, you got in big trouble. Since we weren't in on those conversations, we often did not know of cases of adultery, incest, molestation, domestic violence, or rape that may have occurred. Sometimes the older kids would hear rumors, but it was not something we were informed about. If it happened, more than likely it did not spread beyond the family and definitely not beyond the town. Probably like any other place, some of these things were happening, but we were not privy to them. Because so many people were related, the boys used to tease that they had to leave the county to find someone to date and marry.

When my younger brother Joe was born (at home, of course), I was put outside the house. For some reason, I was not at school that day. I don't know whether it was to stay with Madear so I could get the midwife if the birth started or what. Regardless of the reason for being there, I was banned from the house until after the baby was born. I was allowed back in the house after the birth and was even allowed to name the baby. You can thank me later, Joe Edward.

Growing up in the South could be a dangerous experience. Being poor and Black pushed us further down the proverbial "totem pole". We knew there was racial discrimination locally, at the state level, and at the national level; however, I think our parents shielded us from a lot of the racism. We were also probably shielded in some degree because we were a large family and did not have the transportation to get to and from events addressing this discrimination and outward abuse. Secondly, with their limited education, my parents were not as socially active as some others were. Because of the time consumed in the day-to-day operation of the farm, rearing a large family, and working in the church, they had little spare time. Although not active participants, we were called upon to pray for social and economic improvements.

Once an immediate call went out for the Black people in our community to come together and pray as several Black activists had been arrested and taken to jail in neighboring Rankin County. They had a reputation at that time of being far worse than our own Simpson County in its treatment of Black people in general and specifically black prisoners. Effectual, fervent intercession was made and after being physically abused (I heard some had forks stuck up their nose), they emerged from that jail alive. The call went out to boycott the stores in Mendenhall. As a child, I didn't know and wasn't involved in a lot of these activities, so I don't know firsthand how long or how effective the boycott was. I do know that discrimination did not end then or there.

One of Daddy's sisters, Aunt Mamie, and her husband Uncle Charlie, were actively involved in the civil rights movement in the Hattiesburg, Mississippi area. I did not know this as a child and only found out how involved they were when I became an adult.

The year 1970 brought an end to life as we had known it. With the end of segregated public schools on the horizon, a whole new set of challenges emerged for this GRITS. This would also prove to be my last year of high school, entering the "real" world as a young adult, and getting ready to face adult challenges. Since a lot of people were opposed to integration and equal rights, the civil rights movement became even more heated and open discrimination loomed in the South. Somehow we made it.

Regardless of situations and circumstances or any achievement that I may attain, I realize that nothing achieved in this world can compare to my relationship with God. I value that relationship more than anything else. When I am overwhelmed by the challenges that I encounter in life, I am reminded of my favorite Scriptures which I embrace daily as the guide to my way of living - my actions, conduct, and attitude:

Philippians 4:13 - I can do all things through Christ which strengthens me.

Romans 8:38-39 -For I am persuaded that neither death, nor life, nor angels, nor principalities, nor powers, nor things present, nor things to come, nor height, nor depth, nor any other creature shall be able to separate us from the love of God which is in Christ Jesus our Lord.

Knowing not just who I am but Whose I am has made all the difference!!

Remember to pray always!
If not that the situation changes,
but that God changes us to
deal with the situation.

AND

Plan while you Pray
(It wasn't raining when Noah built the Ark)

Author Ruby Banks Allen

ACKNOWLEDGMENT

My sincere thanks to my support team of family and friends. First of all, let me say thank you for being who you are since many of the stories in this book are about you. Without your antics and pranks, some of these things would not have been possible. Thank you for showing me love and support down through the years, and sometimes that unwanted nudge prompting me to step out of my comfort zone and explore the unknown. These lifetime memories I will cherish forever.

DESCRIPTIVE PHOTOS & CREDITS

Butter churn ;
MS Agriciulture & Forestry
Museum, Jackson, MS

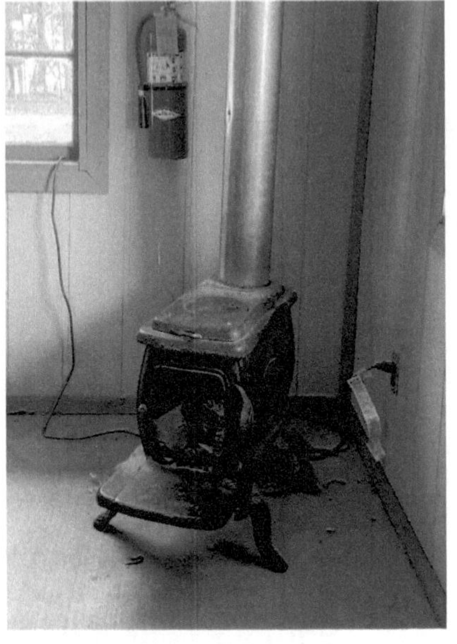

Wood Heater ;
MS Agriciulture & Forestry
Museum, Jackson, MS

Black Pot;
MS Agriciulture & Forestry
Museum, Jackson, MS

Wash Basin;
MS Agriciulture & Forestry
Museum, Jackson, MS

Slop Jar; Enamel Bucket with Lid – Sold on Etsy

Meat Grinder; Creative Commons

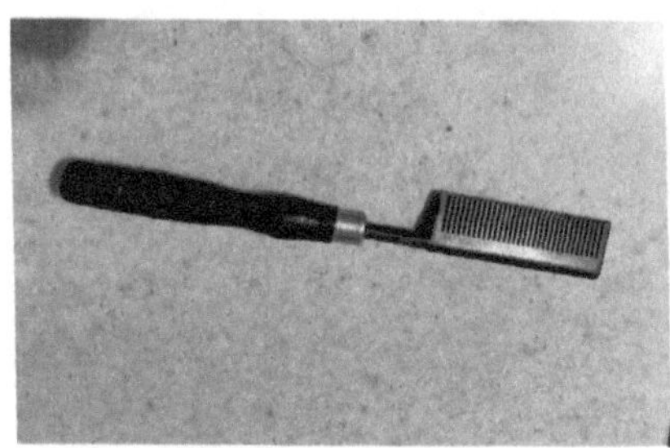

Straightening Comb; Property of my sister Mary

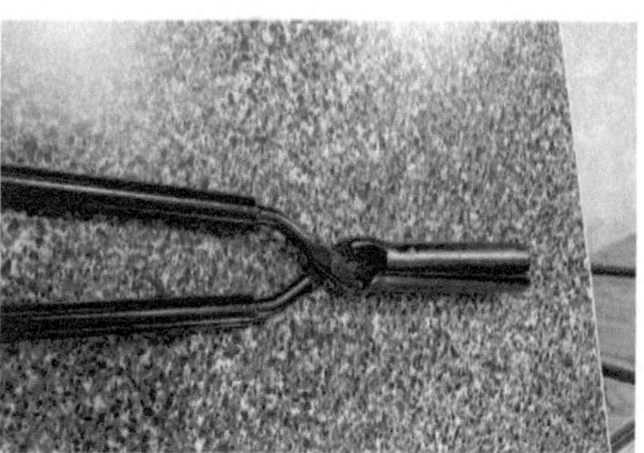

Curling Iron; Inherited from my Aunt Can (Mary)

Number 3 Tub; For Sale by Village Tub and Baths

Cotton Planter; MS Agriciulture & Forestry Museum, Jackson, MS

Quilting Frame ;
MS Agriciulture & Forestry
Museum, Jackson, MS

Quilting Frame Up
Uploaded by Kay Coward
on Google.com

Dipper ; Ebay cookware
collection.com

Water Pail; Ebay cookware
collection.com

My personal sewing
machine inherited from
Aunt Can (Mary)

My personal sewing
machine inherited from
Aunt Can (Mary)

Vintage Washboard; MS Agriciulture & Forestry Museum, Jackson, MS

Outhouse; MS Agriculture & Forestry Museum, Jackson,MS

Washing Machine; For sale on eBay.com

Washing Machine on Bing.com

Hog Trough; For sale on Ebay.co.uk "Poultry and Waterfowl Supplies for Sale"

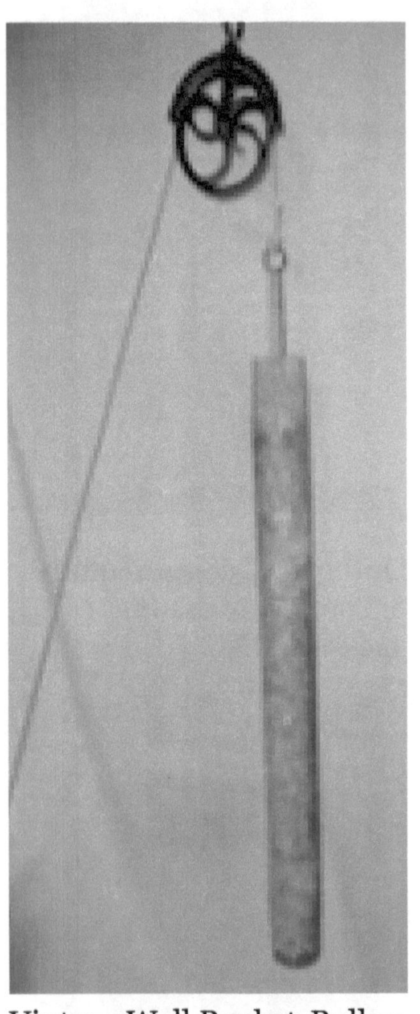

Vintage Well Bucket-Pulley
& Rope; http://www.
Worthport.com

Well Water Cylinder;
"Lehman's Own Galvanized
Well Bucket" lehmans.com

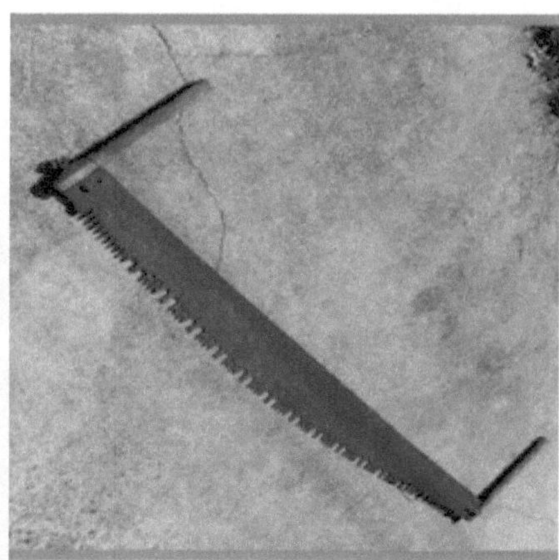

Antiquee Two-man Crosscut Saw; Bing.com/images

Found on Microsoft Bing for sale – Antique Chifferobe with mirror – www.pintrest.com – https://pelaburemasperak.com Best Collection – Antique Chifferobe with mirror

Buck Saw; https:www.acehardware.com/lawnandgarden

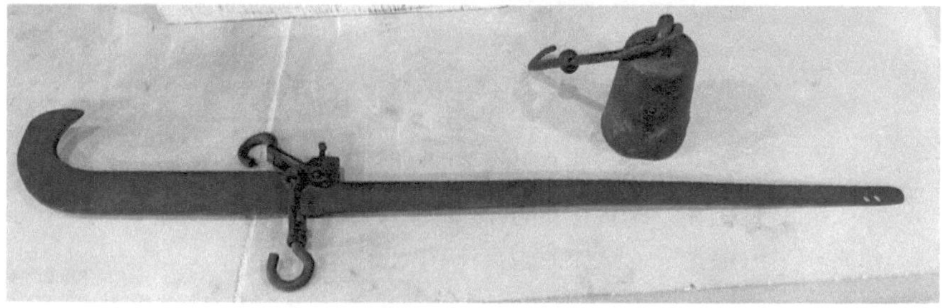

Antique Cotton Scales and Weights (Pea); For Sale on www.ebay.com

Smoke House; MS Agriculture and Forestry Museum, Jackson, MS

Mule Drawn Plow; MS Agriculture and Forestry Museum – Jackson, MS